# STORIES, SPORTS, AND SONGS

Tales and Tunes by a Play by Play Lifer

## BILL SCHOENING

*Stories, Sports, and Songs*

Copyright © 2022 Bill Schoening

All rights reserved

Published by Red Penguin Books

Bellerose Village, New York

Library of Congress Control Number: 2022903438

ISBN

Print 979-8-20139-092-1/978-1-63777-232-4 / 978-1-63777-233-1 / 978-1-63777-715-2

Digital 978-1-63777-234-8

No part of this book may be reproduced in any form or by any electronic or mechanical means, including information storage and retrieval systems, without written permission from the author, except for the use of brief quotations in a book review.

# Contents

In Praise of "Stories, Sports, and Songs" — vii
Preface — ix

1. "Because this is history" — 1
2. Sandlot — 3
3. Connie Mack Stadium — 7
4. Philly Soul — 9
5. Saturdays at the Benn — 11
6. Nuns and Elbows — 13
7. The Cathedral of College Basketball — 17
8. "This ain't a beauty contest" — 21
9. 6'5 and Under — 25
10. City of Brotherly Hoops — 29
11. The Boss Arrives — 31
12. The Secret Kidd — 35
13. Change of Plans — 39
14. AAB — 41
15. Culture Shock — 45
16. A disastrous debut — 47
17. What Blizzard? — 49
18. Nuptials after the deadbeat dad — 51
19. Go west young man — 57
20. I'm a Yankee? — 59
21. The Spanish Mass — 61
22. "I just want to call Agnes" — 63
23. Gelding for Sale — 65
24. Live from the Janitor's Closet — 67
25. The College Try — 69
26. Back to the newsroom — 71
27. Chatting it up with a serial killer — 73
28. "The Voice of Death" — 77
29. High Towering Drive — 79

| | |
|---|---|
| 30. Dizzy Lizzy Strikes | 81 |
| 31. Saving the KSAM Car | 83 |
| 32. Montana State 52 Sam Houston State 48 | 85 |
| 33. "Quasi/ Pseudo Division I" | 87 |
| 34. George | 89 |
| 35. The Pig at Howard Payne | 91 |
| 36. Early Worm | 95 |
| 37. "I'm Here All Week" | 99 |
| 38. The break I needed | 101 |
| 39. LBJ calling | 105 |
| 40. Sportstalk with BS | 107 |
| 41. Spitfire Boss | 109 |
| 42. Coach Gus | 111 |
| 43. "Who's on third?" | 115 |
| 44. "..and now a High Mass…" | 117 |
| 45. Oh…Hi Lesley | 119 |
| 46. "How Can a Guy?" | 123 |
| 47. "Call Me Chi Chi" | 125 |
| 48. The real Chi Chi | 127 |
| 49. "The hardest working man in show business" | 129 |
| 50. Majerus | 135 |
| 51. Tubbs | 137 |
| 52. Zonk | 139 |
| 53. The Lost weekend | 145 |
| 54. Daryl Hamilton | 149 |
| 55. Mackovic | 153 |
| 56. Two places at once | 157 |
| 57. Spike | 159 |
| 58. Fourth and inches | 161 |
| 59. The Zone | 163 |
| 60. Austin Ice Bats | 167 |
| 61. Run Run Ricky | 171 |
| 62. Earl | 173 |
| 63. LaFave | 175 |
| 64. "Me and Daddy" | 181 |
| 65. Turning Down Nadia | 183 |
| 66. Ditka's Autograph | 185 |

| | |
|---|---:|
| 67. Major | 189 |
| 68. Lucchesi–Party of 10 | 191 |
| 69. Inspirational No-hitter | 193 |
| 70. How Far is Heaven? | 195 |
| 71. "You're getting a call tonight" | 199 |
| 72. Philly Billy | 203 |
| 73. Tony Senior | 207 |
| 74. Manu Voodoo | 211 |
| 75. Jimmy Chang | 217 |
| 76. Lambeau | 219 |
| 77. Beno | 221 |
| 78. The Spurs Melting Pot | 223 |
| 79. What's Your Title again? | 227 |
| 80. Red Rocket | 229 |
| 81. Chillin' at Churchill | 233 |
| 82. Blame it on Springsteen | 237 |
| 83. This place gives me the creeps | 239 |
| 84. "That's how ya got it" | 243 |
| 85. Redemption Season | 245 |
| 86. Iceman | 247 |
| 87. Boban | 249 |
| 88. Epinal | 253 |
| 89. Ego deflation | 259 |
| 90. The West Catholic Hall of Fame | 261 |
| 91. The Mitt | 265 |
| 92. Kairos | 267 |
| 93. Points Galore | 273 |
| 94. Comebacks | 275 |
| 95. Milestones | 279 |
| 96. All 50 Club | 283 |
| 97. Streak Stopper | 285 |
| 98. "Here Comes Smokin' Joe" | 287 |
| 99. A Lost Night in Mexico City | 289 |
| 100. Cruising the Rhine | 291 |
| A few extras while I got ya… | 293 |
| Epilogue | 297 |

Acknowledgments 299
About the Author 301

## In Praise of "Stories, Sports, and Songs"

"A cinematic portrayal of Philly neighborhood life (including catching elbows from a nun nicknamed Big John) to handicapping lessons from his dad at the track, to career advice from a young singer named Springsteen, it's all a joyride of a read, about a life Bill could not have plotted out if he tried."

~ Mike Jensen, College Basketball Writer Philadelphia Inquirer

"Don't miss this opportunity for a glimpse into the world of an amazing storyteller. Bill Schoening's stories are some of the most interesting, insightful, and humorous that I've ever heard. He takes you on to the field and into the arena to relay fun anecdotes from his sportscasting career."

~ Sean Elliott,   College Basketball Hall of Famer and NBA Champion

"This book is a fantastic read.  I loved it. Great stories from a well-rounded broadcaster and entertainer!"

~ J.T. the Brick , Nationally syndicated talk show host

# Preface

As I sit down to start this project, I'm wondering on one hand why I've decided to write and share my stories. On the other hand, I'm also wondering why it has taken me so long. For years, I've had friends and colleagues tell me I should write a book, some of them in jest, but some seriously. What I've tried to do here is recall, to the best of my ability, anecdotes about my true life experiences. The stories will take you around the globe and introduce you to some friends, acquaintances, and other folks with whom I have crossed a path or two. You'll go from the exhilarating scenery of National Parks to the dark desolation and sweltering conditions of a maximum-security prison in Texas. Some stories are funny, while others are a bit darker in nature. Some may even be thought-provoking. I've been in radio for over four decades, so there will be some tales about life on the air as well. I also include the lyrics to a dozen of the songs I've written. Before we get to these tales, allow me to start my story at the beginning of my journey. I was the fifth and final child of Bill and Peggy Schoening, born on November 4th, 1958 in the Misericordia Hospital in Philadelphia. My dad, Bill Schoening Sr, was a fun-loving, hard-drinking breadman, delivering cakes, bread, donuts and pastries to doorsteps throughout our neighborhood. His route covered all of Southwest Philly. When I was twelve years old, he switched careers, leaving Bond Baking Company to become a bartender at Hastings Café.

My dad knew triumphs and tragedies. He was almost killed in the South Pacific in May of 1945, when two Japanese kamikaze pilots flew into the USS Drexler, a destroyer patrolling off Okinawa. 159 of his shipmates died. Four months earlier his younger brother Thomas, a Private First Class in the U.S. Army's 12th Armored Division, was killed in action in eastern France. Those two incidents stayed with my dad until he died in 1988. Just prior to the war, my dad married Peggy McCarty, a pretty Irish girl who came from a poor family in South Philly. My mom was 39 years old when I came along. Throughout my early childhood and developmental years, my mom was my greatest supporter, making sure I had everything I needed, even though money was very tight. Apparently, when she announced her pregnancy it was a bit of a shock. Some would call me a mistake baby. When I was 18, I asked my dad why there were six years between my sister Chrissie and me. "Billy," he explained, "I swear I don't know how you happened. I must have bumped into your mother in the hallway one night." My dad was a real character. I'll tell you more about him later. Even though I grew up in a tough city neighborhood, I was surrounded by love and encouragement. We didn't have much money, but my buddies and I were too busy playing sports to notice.

I grew up in a very modest row home at 6932 Chelwynde Avenue, literally around the corner from Finnegan Recreation Center, a sprawling property (at least for the inner city) that featured six baseball diamonds, two football fields, two basketball courts, a swimming pool, and five tennis courts. They even had a bocce court for the older Italian-American gentlemen in the neighborhood. I'd watch them sometimes and try to pick up an Italian curse word or two. When I was 10 years old, I remember listening to an old Philco Radio in the middle bedroom of our house. I shared the room with my older brother Tom, who was in the United States Air Force at the time, stationed in Kunsan, South Korea. I was falling asleep one night, listening to Byrum Saam broadcast the Phillies-Giants game from Candlestick Park in San Francisco, and I had a moment of clarity. I decided that night, at the age of ten, I was going to be a play-by-play announcer. It was the summer of 1969. A few months after I told my mom about my career goals, she cashed in some books of S&H Green Stamps to buy me a reel-to-reel tape recorder, complete with a microphone! I was on my way. I'd imitate ABC's Howard Cosell and Phillies announcer Byrum Saam, do impromptu comedy bits with my friend Paul Dever, who had a background in theatre, and on more than one occasion, I would turn down Curt Gowdy and Tony Kubek on the NBC Game of the week, and record my own version of the Yankees-Red Sox game.

This would be a common theme for me over the next ten years. I would imagine how I would call a play every time I watched a game. Even when I played first base for West Catholic High, I had a running play-by-play in my mind. It kept me in tune to the game and focused. To this day, I try to approach each game with that same mindset – to be locked in.

It was from this early juncture that I started thinking like a play-by-play announcer. As I got into the radio business and eventually climbed the play-by-play ladder, I reminded myself of where this whole dream started - in a small bedroom in a row home in Southwest Philly. My journey has taken me from calling games for a local High School in west Texas (Lamesa High) to small college (Sam Houston State) to major college (University of Texas) to the NBA (San Antonio Spurs). I consider myself very blessed to have been able to take a step up each time.

I am far from perfect and have made mistakes through the years, but I do have faith in God and firmly believe that I have had a guardian angel guiding me, keeping me out of harm's way to navigate this path from inner-city playground kid to a guy that has called four NBA Championships. I've been able to visit all 50 states and have broadcast games in 40 of them. During my tenure with the San Antonio Spurs, I've called games in Mexico, Canada, France, Germany and Turkey. Along the way, I've been able to meet some fascinating folks, and visit some incredible places. These are the reasons I felt compelled to share some of these tales. Whether you've never heard a single broadcast of mine or you go back to my Texas Longhorn days or earlier, I sincerely hope you enjoy "Stories, Sports and Songs."

Peggy McCarty married Bill Schoening Sr. on September 21st, 1940.
I didn't come along for another 18 years.

# 1

## "Because this is history"

My earliest childhood memory is walking hand in hand with my mom as she did her shopping on Elmwood Avenue, about a two-block walk from our house. I had just turned five years old and was attending kindergarten classes in the morning at Patterson School. On a Friday in November, my mom picked me up at the school around noontime, and we walked up to the supermarket. I recall her making me walk on the outside. "Always remember to be a gentleman and walk on the outside near the street whenever you are walking with a girl or a lady," she told me. From that day on, I have not felt comfortable walking with a female companion unless she is on the inside.

As we were about to check out of the store, I remember a sense of commotion. The cashier then told my mom that she had just heard on the radio that President Kennedy had been shot in Dallas. My mom became visibly upset, she quickly paid the cashier, and we hurried back home. As we watched the events of that tragic day unfold on our black and white television set, I distinctly remember being disappointed that Casper the Friendly Ghost and my other favorite cartoons were being preempted by coverage of the assassination.

When I asked my mom why the cartoons hadn't come on yet, she stopped sobbing for a moment, and said, "…because this is history." Like many Catholic families in the neighborhood, we had a portrait of JFK displayed in our house, right next to a picture of Pope Paul VI. I tried to console my mom, but that was nearly impossible. After all, the president was young, handsome, Irish Catholic, and had served in the U.S. Navy during WWII. Many years later, when I visited the Sixth Floor Museum in Dealey Plaza in Dallas, I was brought back to the day when a five-year-old kid in Philly tried to comfort his mom while wondering if the cartoons would ever come on.

## 2

# Sandlot

By the time I was seven years old I was playing hardball. The organized little league at Finnegan Playground started out with 10 to 12 year olds, so that would have to wait. Frankie Sands was two years older than me and lived right behind us, across the alley. Frankie had a shopping cart full of old baseballs, bats, beat-up gloves, and even some antiquated catcher's equipment. He organized what he called a "street team" and he would challenge other ragtag teams of kids our age to play seven-inning games down at Finnegan Playground. If you've ever seen the movie "The Sandlot," it was very similar to that.

We didn't have uniforms or cleats, and there was very little adult supervision. I was one of the youngest kids on the team, but I always had a spot, usually at first base. I was left-handed, a little pudgy and didn't run very fast, but Frankie liked the way I hit the ball and he always included me. Playing with the older kids helped me improve. Around this time I had a friend named Dennis McFadden, whose dad Hugh loved to hit us grounders, pop-ups and fly balls. I would spend hours at the playground going through fielding drills. Thanks to the sandlot games and those hours with Mr. McFadden, I talked my dad into letting me try out for the 10-12 team sponsored by The Catholic War Veterans, or CWV. I was a year too young. Mr. Bill Liscio, the head coach, was skeptical at first but gave me a tryout. It went well. I was the starting first baseman for that team for the next three seasons.

My dad was so proud he went out and got me an expensive first baseman's mitt. I couldn't believe he spent $20, which seemed like a lot of money to me. Box seats to the Phillies games cost $3.25, so I was very proud of that glove. I treated it like a baby. I even slept with it under my pillow to help break it in. The following spring I served as the batboy for West Catholic High. West played their varsity games on Field #1 at Finnegan, about 200 yards from my house. I vowed to myself that one day I would play first base for West Catholic. That dream came true seven years later. By the way, Frankie Sands, the kid behind the alley who organized those sandlot games, became a coxswain for the champion West Catholic Crew team. In the late 70s, I heard he accepted the head coaching position for the Crew team at the University of Nebraska. That was the last I heard of him until one night in 1998. I was at a sports bar in Lincoln the night before a Texas at Nebraska football game. The bar was packed with Cornhusker sports memorabilia. Just above my spot at the bar was a boat oar, signed by the Cornhusker Rowing squad. Most prevalent was the autograph of their head coach, Frankie Sands.

*My young life was totally consumed by playing sports.*

# 3

## Connie Mack Stadium

My dad worked strange hours delivering for the Bond Baking Company. He'd get up at 3:30 in the morning, drive to West Philly to the Bond Plant, and load up his truck for deliveries. He then drove all through our neighborhood, delivering the baked goods to families. My friends called my dad "Bill the Breadman." He was a hard worker who also played hard. He was a shot and a beer guy who liked to play cards and the ponies. He also loved baseball and one Tuesday in the summer of 1965 he announced to my mom, "I'm taking the kid to the Phillies game." I was thrilled. We then made the long drive up to North Philly.

It seemed like we'd never get there, but when we did it was worth the wait. When we walked through the portals and saw the field for the first time, I was like a little kid. Wait, I was a little kid! I couldn't believe how green the manicured lawn was that served as the infield and outfield. In right-center, there was a huge scoreboard with a massive "Longines" clock at the very top. Ballantine Beer had a banner ad just below the clock. This was so much different from a grainy black and white TV picture. The LA Dodgers road grays were crisp and professional, and the

Phillies wore home whites with bright red pinstripes. I caught a glimpse of Phillies outfielder Johnny Callison as he trotted to the outfield to do some stretching. I had his Topps card!

This was too good to be true. My dad knew a guy who worked as an attendant in the press box and he allowed us to sit in the writers' section during batting practice. From that vantage point, I thought every ball hit was going to leave the park. Most were just routine fly balls. I already loved baseball, but going to that game got me hooked. Through the years, my dad and I had a few disagreements, but we could always enjoy going to the ballgame. It also started a streak. I had seen the Phillies play at least one game for 55 consecutive seasons. The streak ended when COVID hit in 2020.

# 4

# Philly Soul

My first exposure to music was seeing the colorful posters of Motown artists on the wall of my bedroom. My brother Tom loved soul music, especially Smokey Robinson, The Temptations, and The Four Tops. He left a few 45 rpm singles behind when he enlisted in the Air Force in 1967. I used to play them on my sister's little record player with tiny speakers. While Tom was away, a unique R&B sound started coming out of our hometown. Artists like the Delfonics, the Stylistics, Labelle, and Billy Paul were recording hits, but my favorite was Harold Melvin and the Blue Notes. The lead singer of that band, Teddy Pendergrass, is the most underrated soul singer ever. Of course, that is a biased opinion because Teddy is from Philly, but do yourself a favor when you're in a mellow mood and listen to "If You Don't Know Me By Now."

Teddy sang with a depth and emotion that drew me in. I remember walking up to Jolley Records on Woodland Avenue and buying singles for 85 cents. I always made sure I had some Philly Soul in my 45's collection. At Finnegan playground, where I spent many days and nights, there was a group that sang a capella. They called themselves "The Sons of Robin Stone." I can recall one chilly night in early December of my eighth-grade year. I got done my shooting drills at the outdoor court and started the short walk home. Just inside the gate to the playground, huddled closely together, were the Sons of Robin Stone, practicing their harmonies. I stayed and listened to a few tunes. These cats could really sing.

They eventually went into the studio and recorded some songs, two of which got airplay in Philly, "Love is Just Around the Corner" and "Got to Get You Back." I thought both tunes were good enough to be hits. As we all know, the music business is unforgiving and the Sons of Robin Stone never made it, but they captured the spirit of Philly Soul and they gave it a shot. The songs I write these days tend to feature more of an Americana/Folk feel, but deep in my DNA, there is an abundance of Philly Soul. My most recent song, "Here Comes Smokin' Joe" pays homage to my Philly roots.

# 5

## Saturdays at the Benn

About a mile from our house was Woodland Avenue, a wide street that was a beehive of activity in the '60s. The Avenue featured shops, restaurants, department stores, and two vaudeville era theaters, the Benn and the Benson. The Benn Theater, which opened in 1923, hosted a doubleheader movie matinee on Saturdays. Neighborhood kids flocked to the place to get a full day of entertainment for 25 cents. My closest sibling in age was my sister Chrissie, who has always been a loving, supporting and kind sibling. She was six years older than me but allowed me to tag along on those days when I wasn't playing baseball. I was probably six or seven years old.

It was then that I fell in love with going to the movies. At first, I think it was the popcorn and the huge screen, but I also enjoyed the storyline, the acting, and the music. The Saturday twin shows did not necessarily feature current films of the day. I remember seeing Charlton Heston in "The Ten Commandments," Kirk Douglas in "Spartacus" and Gregory Peck in "How the West Was Won." Those movies sparked a love of cinema for me that still is burning today.

I love all kinds of films but am especially drawn to period pieces. In recent years I find myself watching lots of documentaries and foreign films. Since my dad fought in WWII, I have a keen interest in films about the war. My family doesn't quite understand my fascination. If my son Karl walks into the room and I am watching yet another film about WWII, he always says, "Dad, I'll save you some time. The Nazis lost."

## 6

## Nuns and Elbows

I must admit that attending Catholic School for 12 years had a profound impact on me. Most of it was pretty positive; some not so much. There always seemed to be order and organization, and those were good things. The first eight years of my education I attended St. Clement's Grade School, which was run by the Sisters of the Immaculate Heart of Mary. They lived in a convent adjacent to the school. Most of the sisters were good teachers and fostered a caring attitude. There were several nuns, however, that practiced intimidation and corporal punishment to keep order in the classroom.

The worst of these was my 7th-grade teacher for math, Sister Marita John. We all feared "Big Bad John," her nickname earned from the old Jimmy Dean country song. It was later shortened to just "Big John." I'm sure Sister Marita John had days when she was pleasant and kind, but I can't recall any. She always had a scowl on her face and I was convinced each day she would look at the class roster and figure out which student had not yet incurred her wrath. I was a pretty good student but was guilty of being a class clown on occasion. However, I was always on my best behavior in Big John's class. This woman intimidated the hell out of me.

One day in March, I had a difficult time figuring out a math equation at my desk. When she asked for a volunteer to put the equation up on the board and solve it, I didn't raise my hand. At that point, she must have figured I was overdue for a whacking. She selected me. My knees were shaking on the way to the huge blackboard that was maybe 12 feet wide. As I started to work my way through the problem, I was getting a weird feeling. On the second line of the problem, I got stuck, and couldn't figure out the next step…then…BOOM! The fiercest right elbow of all time came crashing across the back of my head, projecting my face directly into the chalkboard. If Sister Marita John was a player in the NHL, she would've received two minutes for elbowing and an additional two minutes for roughing.

I could hear the oohs and aahs of my fellow students. Tears filled my eyes but I couldn't cry. I had a crush on at least two girls in that class! As I reached up to see if I was bleeding from the nose, I got another elbow, but this was just a glancing blow that barely caught the top of my head. Then Big John gave it to me verbally, yelling, "Don't pick your nose in front of my class! You're not so popular now, are you?" She sent me back to my seat, telling the class that I apparently must think I'm a lot smarter than I actually am. After that day I was relieved because I took her best shot, and I figured she was through with me. It was just simply my turn that day. I was right; she never laid another hand on me.

To this day at our grade school reunions, stories abound of Sister Marita John. I do have some good memories of that period, mostly because of basketball. I also smile when I recall the 8th grade dances, which is when most of us started to discover girls. The boys hung on one side of the dance floor and the girls on the other. When it came to slow dances, guys had to be careful.

You don't want to get shot down in front of the entire class. At the time I liked a girl named Cheryl Hopper, who was one of the smartest girls in the class. I was a bit nervous, but Cheryl said yes when I asked for a dance, Our first slow song was Procol Harum's "Whiter Shade of Pale." I had no idea what I was doing, and the dance turned out to be a five-minute hug with bad foot movement. Cheryl was very nice but politely told me I was "bouncing."

I guess I started to shuffle more than bounce after that, but I did get a five-minute hug with a pretty girl, and that was good enough for me. When I returned to the boy's side after the song, Sister Miriam (who was much nicer than Big John) took me aside and whispered, "William, the next time you dance with Cheryl, please leave a little room for the Holy Spirit."

# 7

# The Cathedral of College Basketball

Until my brother Tom returned home from his four-year stint in the Air Force, I had not attended a lot of live basketball games. I loved the sport and played organized basketball through 8th grade, but my dad was never a fan of hoops and had no interest. My brother-in-law Joe Antonelli took me to a few 76ers games, but by the 1972-73 season (my 8th-grade year) the Sixers were really bad. They had traded my favorite player of all time (Wilt Chamberlain) to the Lakers, and that started a decline. They won only 9 games in '72-73 (an all-time worst in NBA history) but I do remember getting to see the Milwaukee Bucks with Kareem Abdul Jabbar and Oscar Robertson.

Shortly after Tom got back to Philly, he started taking me to games at the Palestra, the home gym for the University of Pennsylvania. The Palestra, built in 1927, has been called The Cathedral of College Basketball. I think I was 13-years-old the first time I walked into this unique place. It is simple but grand. Painted wooden benches make up the vast majority of the 8,722 seats that rise up to iron rafters high above the playing surface. Not only did the Penn Quakers of the Ivy League play their home games at the Palestra, but the other four NCAA Division

One schools in Philly (Temple, LaSalle, St. Joseph's and Villanova) also played some games there.

Saturday doubleheaders during this era were a real treat. Although it was not recognized as an official NCAA conference, the city teams formed the Big Five, and whenever there was a City Series game, the tension was palpable and the place was packed. High school basketball playoff games were also held at the Palestra. In March of 1976, during my junior year, I was on hand as Bishop Kenrick defeated my school, West Catholic, for the Catholic League championship.

During the game, I recall imagining how I might describe the action on the radio. I then thought to myself, "Maybe one day I'll get to call a game here." The concourse of the Palestra features a priceless collection of memorabilia from years gone by. Old warm-ups, uniforms, and trophies are displayed in large glass cases. The vintage photographs of future Hall of Famers in their high school and college days are outstanding. There's Wilt Chamberlain of Overbrook, Kobe Bryant of Lower Merion, Jerry West of West Virginia, and Calvin Murphy of Niagara. These are just a few that come to mind. All of these players flashed their early skills at the Palestra.

In the summer of 2012, while vacationing in Philly, my son Karl asked me if he could see the Palestra. I called my friend Dan Harrell, who for two decades basically ran the place. Dan was the custodian and caretaker of the building and no one ever loved the Palestra more than Dan. He enthusiastically said yes. After the tour, we were about to leave, and Dan called me into his office and said he had a little surprise for me. He reached into a drawer at his desk and handed me a piece of wood about eight inches long and two inches wide. It was a piece of the original floor from 1927! It remains one of my favorite keepsakes.

When I returned to Austin, I enlisted the help of a trophy shop to cut the plank into four pieces, and then each piece was mounted on a marble plaque. On each plaque was engraved, "This is a piece of the original floor of the historic Palestra in Philadelphia, Pennsylvania, built in 1927. More college games have been played at the Palestra than any gym in the United States." I kept one plaque for myself, and then gave one to my brother Tom, for the many cold nights we'd go watch games there. One went to former Spurs forward Malik Rose, who attended Drexel University, which is adjacent to Penn. Malik played many games and often practiced at the Palestra. The other plaque went to Spurs Head Coach Gregg Popovich, who has always had a fondness for the history of the game. Pop loves the Palestra and has conducted game-day shootarounds there. He also has a longtime friendship with former Penn and Temple Coach Fran Dunphy.

Late in 2015, I got a call from Brian Seltzer, at the time the Voice of the Penn Quakers. He asked if I would be interested in calling the Ivy League opener between Princeton and Penn at the Palestra. The Spurs had an off day but were playing on Monday night in Brooklyn against the Nets. So, instead of flying with the team to New York, I booked a commercial flight to Philly. Brother Tom picked me up, we grabbed lunch, and then I got to call the game alongside former Penn great Stan Pawlak. Princeton won the game in overtime, but it was an absolute thrill to broadcast a game in an arena that held so many memories for me.

After the game, Tom dropped me off at the 30th Street Train Station, which is less than a mile from the Penn Campus. I took the train up to NYC, met up with the Spurs, and called the NBA game in Brooklyn on Monday. Sometimes I feel like I should pinch myself to make sure this isn't all a dream. Oh, and to top it off, two weeks later I got a check for $250 from the University of Pennsylvania for the broadcast. I had totally forgotten I was going to get paid for that gig!

## 8

## "This ain't a beauty contest"

When I was in 6th grade, my dad thought I had come of age enough to go to the horse track with him. One of the first things I noticed was the clientele was different than at a baseball game. There were very few women at the track in those days, and there was certainly more of a "seedy" element. Just about everybody was smoking pipes, cigarettes or cigars. Shots and beers were being consumed. Frustrated gamblers were dejectedly tossing losing tickets to the floor. Not surprisingly, I heard some very salty language.

However, I loved seeing the horses up close and enjoyed going out to the rail to see the post parade prior to each race. On that first day at the races, I pointed out a beautiful gray horse to my dad and told him I liked the number 7 horse in the upcoming race. He then looked at the racing program and showed me the recent history of this attractive gray horse. He had finished 5th, 4th, and 8th in his previous three races. Then he looked at me, handed me the program, and said, "Don't pick a pretty one, pick a fast one. This ain't a beauty contest."

He then proceeded to show me how to read the racing form. He usually handed me a $20 bill for the day. He'd tell me, "10 races,

$2 a race. Plus I'll buy your popcorn and cokes." I was very happy with that. One Sunday night at Brandywine Park in Delaware, my mom came along. Before the second race, she announced out loud that she liked the #4 horse, Anchor W, because my dad was in the Navy and his first name was William. I then pointed out to mom that this horse was inconsistent and had not finished in the top three in four straight races.

She then punched my dad on the arm and said, "Math is his least favorite subject in school, but he can read this shit upside down." Those early days with my dad were bonding for us, but I'm so happy neither of my sons got the itch for the horses like I did. I will admit that for a while I was going to the track too much, always blaming my dad's genes. There was a small track east of Austin called Manor Downs that was open for simulcast wagering. Manor was the true definition of a small-time race track. Live racing was conducted only a couple of weekends a season, just so they could keep their license.

Early in my tenure with the Spurs, I frequented the place on off days on a regular basis so I could bet tracks from around the country. I never bet a lot of money; I just liked the action, I guess. Anyway, one random Wednesday I was headed to Manor Downs to bet on Philly Park, Delaware Park, and Aqueduct. On the way, I was listening to nationally syndicated talk show host Jim Rome. At one point on my drive, about two minutes from the entrance to the track, Rome started talking about horse racing in general, and gamblers, in particular. He basically said that if it's opening day at Del Mar or a Saturday afternoon during the Triple Crown races - it's okay to visit the horse track. However, if there's someone listening to this show right now and you're headed to some small-time, hole-in-the-wall track with a bar and a few TVs, you just may be a degenerate. It was as if Rome was looking at me through my car radio. After laughing out loud I yelled at Rome, "Guilty as charged, I must be a degenerate!" I'm happy to report that I only visit the track on rare occasions these days, and when I do, I still blame it on my dad's genes.

# 9

## 6'5 and Under

By the time my high school years rolled around, I concentrated only on playing baseball and tennis, but I had a deep love for basketball. I contemplated trying out for the freshman team at West, but I was only about 5'8 at the time, not nearly big enough for the frontcourt, and not quite quick enough for the backcourt. I was hoping to stay close to the game in some way. Here's where my brother helped out once again. The City of Philadelphia Department of Recreation had just begun a program called NYC, which stood for Neighborhood Youth Corps. The purpose of the program was to give low-income inner-city youth summer jobs at Recreation Centers throughout the city.

Tom had begun his career with the Deptartment of Recreation just a few years earlier and was working at McCreesh Playground, a mile from our house. I could've opted to work at Finnegan right around the corner, but I wanted to work with my brother and I knew that the two-mile round trip walk would be good for me each day. The best aspect of my job was keeping the scorebook and the clock at the McCreesh 6'5" and under basketball league. The games, played in the evenings under the lights, featured former high school and college players. Tom served as co-commissioner of the league. I was very impressed with the high level of play.

One of the standout players was sharpshooting guard Fran O'Hanlon, who had played at Villanova, spent one season in the ABA, and then continued his career in Europe. Other Big Five players such as Steve Batory (Penn) and Jim Crawford (LaSalle) raised the bar even higher. The referees in the league were top-notch. Future NBA official Joe Crawford, and highly respected college refs Hank Nichols and Gerry Donaghy brought their whistles and were paying early career dues.

Crawford worked 50 NBA Finals games during a 39-year career. He officiated 374 playoff games, an all-time record. Nichols eventually became the NCAA supervisor of officials, worked 10 Final Fours, and was inducted into the Naismith Memorial Basketball Hall of Fame in 2012. Years later, I got to know Donaghy very well when he worked games in the Big XII Conference during my time calling University of Texas games. His son Tim became an NBA official, but was convicted in a betting scandal, lost his job, and then served 15 months in a federal prison. I always felt bad about that because Gerry was one of the nicest officials I had ever met and I knew how much that entire ordeal must have hurt him.

Gerry Donaghy worked 19 consecutive NCAA tournaments and four Final Fours. These games at McCreesh also drew fans, sometimes as many as 200 sitting on the grassy hill adjacent to the court. Many of them were enjoying malted beverages. I couldn't believe my good fortune once again. Some of my friends were working construction jobs during the summer, digging ditches. Here I was, keeping the scorebook at basketball games. That skill, by the way, became very handy a few years later when I started broadcasting games. Statistics monitors were unheard of in the late '70s and '80s, so I always kept the book while calling the game. That way, I could keep track of individual scorers, fouls, and timeouts. Sitting courtside watching basketball on a warm summer evening was, at least in my mind, the best summer job ever.

---

When I first started taking guitar lessons in the mid 90's, I never dreamed I'd write or co-write over two dozen songs. To be completely honest, I have never taken the time to become a great guitar player, but those early lessons allowed me to improve my sense of melody. The inspiration for writing lyrics and melodies has come from a variety of sources; family, faith, history, relationships, sports, and travel.

The first song I ever wrote was inspired by a poster promoting the upcoming 1996-97 college basketball season at the University of Texas. Guard/Forward Kris Clack was flying through the air for a dunk on an outdoor court at dusk, with the caption "Why Drive When You Can Fly?" I immediately thought to myself that that would be a good song title.

---

*"Why Drive?"*

*The option's open to you   It's time to make up your mind*

*You can go left or right   into the lane you will find*

*Chorus*

*The screen is set   the rim's in sight*

*Why drive when you can fly? Why drive when you can fly?*

*The zone's been shutting us down   we've been missing our threes*

*It's time to get a better look and take it among the trees*

*Repeat Chorus*

*It's time to take it on home  Be sure when you slam it down*

*Who will stop you when you take off?  No one here in this town*

*Repeat Chorus*

10

## City of Brotherly Hoops

By now I had a bad case of Hoops Fever. I wanted to cover basketball. In the first week of my junior year, I met with Mr. Vince Cancro, the moderator for the Blue and White, the annual yearbook. I volunteered my services. I was named sports editor but I would help out in other areas as well. I learned about cropping pictures, layout, design, and editing copy. I also approached Mr. Bob Crewalk, moderator for the West Catholic News, the campus newspaper that was printed about every two weeks. I told him of my various interests and for the next two years I would write features about sports and music. In addition to playing varsity baseball, I would pour my heart into the Yearbook and Newspaper, working on skills that would be very helpful in my career down the line.

I could not have picked a better time to be covering high school basketball in the city. There were awesome players everywhere. At West Catholic, we had forward Michael Brooks, a future NBA lottery pick who starred at LaSalle University and became that school's all-time leading scorer, until Lionel Simmons broke Brooks' record. Overbrook High featured Lewis Lloyd, who played at Drake University and averaged 30 points and 15 rebounds one season. Monsignor Bonner featured Danny Hastings, who played in the Big 10 at Wisconsin, and West Philly had the best high school player I have ever seen, Gene Banks. A 6'7" forward, Banks was an elite athlete, could run the floor, and could score inside and out. He went on to help put Duke on the map (with the help of players like Jim Spanarkel and Mike Gminski). Duke made it to the Final Four in Banks' freshman year, falling to Kentucky in the championship game. Banks was drafted by the San Antonio Spurs and spent 12 seasons in the NBA.

During my senior year, Mr. Cancro taught a class called "Independent Project." Students had a chance to be creative and embark on a project of their own choosing, as long as it was approved by the teacher. Since I wanted to pursue a career in sportscasting, Mr. Cancro gave me the thumbs up. I hosted a weekly sports and music television show (with very rudimentary equipment) during which I interviewed coaches, athletes and musicians. I also got to "broadcast" a West Catholic vs. Roman Catholic basketball game. The first game I ever called was into a Panasonic cassette recorder while sitting on the bleacher steps at the old West Catholic gym.

My color analyst was Ed Downs, who was playing junior college ball at the time, and later played for the Washington Generals, the team that toured with the Harlem Globetrotters. As far as I know, only three people ever heard that tape - Ed, Mr. Cancro, and me. I'm sure it was lacking in quality and I was just figuring out how to describe plays, but I got an "A" in that class and some positive words of encouragement from my teacher. It was a confidence boost for me. It had been eight years since that night I was falling asleep listening to the Phillies game when I decided I wanted to be a play-by-play guy. Now I've actually called a game and got a good review. I knew it was only the beginning, but I was thrilled to take the first step.

## 11

## The Boss Arrives

On more than one occasion in this book, I will reference my English teacher at West, Mr. Paul Grillo. We all called him Mr. G. He wrote poetry, smoked a tobacco pipe, walked like Groucho Marx, and had a bushy mustache. He was the polar opposite of Sister Marita John and some of the nuns at St. Clement's. He also taught a class for upperclassmen called, "The Poetry and Language of Rock and Roll." I thought it was cool that I was attending a school where I could one day take a class analyzing the lyrics of rock songs.

For some reason, Mr. G singled me out during freshman year and would give me albums to take home. He'd tell me to listen closely, take some notes, and then return the LP within a couple of days with an opinion. That's the first time I heard "Greetings from Asbury Park, NJ." I was absolutely blown away by the lyrics, melodies, and musicianship of the E Street Band. I had never heard of Bruce Springsteen before, even though he lived 75 miles from Philly. When I returned the album with rave reviews, Mr. G then gave me a second Springsteen album, the recently released "The Wild, The Innocent, and the E Street Shuffle."

The song "Rosalita" became an instant favorite of mine and I was hooked. Up to that point, I had listened mostly to top 40 and soul on AM Radio. Springsteen changed all of that. Neither of Bruce's first two records sold very well for Columbia, but his performances during live shows were beginning to get attention. My buddy Kurt Titchenell, a trombone player in the West Catholic Jazz Band, loved Springsteen's funky side (especially Clarence Clemmons' saxophone) and was an even bigger fan than me.

Kurt drove a 1965 Mustang with a stick shift. He also had a cool sound system in his car, complete with an 8-track player. I loved hanging with this guy. One summer Saturday, on a complete whim, we drove to the shore and rented a room in an elderly Italian lady's house. I think the room cost $7. Springsteen's buddies, Southside Johnny and the Asbury Jukes, were scheduled to play the Stone Pony that night. The legal drinking age was 18 in New Jersey, but Kurt had an ultra-cool leather jacket and I had a bushy mustache and we approached the door to the club with a Philly swagger. It must've worked because a few minutes later we were inside when the lights came down, the horn section kicked in, and here was Southside Johnny, singing with Bruce Springsteen!

We were hoping Bruce might be hanging out, but we didn't expect him to be playing and singing. It was a very soulful set. During a break, Kurt and I noticed Bruce standing just a few feet from us. He seemed very approachable so we said hi and told him we had driven over from Philly. That was a good icebreaker because Bruce loved our hometown. A disc jockey named Ed Sciaky from WMMR in Philly was one of Bruce's biggest supporters and gave him lots of airplay. We only chatted for a couple of minutes and for some silly reason I asked him if he was making money yet. He then asked me what I wanted to do for a living when I graduated from school. When I told him I hoped to be a sportscaster, he decided to teach me a life lesson, saying, "Making money is not making it, but doing what you love is making it. Go be a sportscaster, and don't worry about the money you make." Those words stayed with me, especially in the early days of my career when I was working long hours for short pay. If I was going to be a successful sportscaster, I was going to have to work my way up. There were no shortcuts.

When Bruce released "Born to Run" in August of 1975, his third album was the charm. The title cut became a huge hit, and in October he graced the covers of Time and Newsweek magazines in the same week! Bruce and the E Street Band had been playing small colleges and clubs in the Philly area, but shortly after "Born to Run" he was booked for a four-night engagement at the Tower Theatre in Upper Darby, a Philly suburb. The shows sold out within hours. I was able to get a single ticket to the first night's show, but Kurt was not. Kurt heard through the grapevine that Bruce was staying at the University Hilton on the Penn Campus. We were hoping we could meet him again, so we hung around the hotel for an hour, and even stopped in the coffee shop and got some ice cream.

As we headed back to the car, a tour bus pulled up and out walked Springsteen and his manager at the time, Mike Appel. There was nobody else around. We tried to play it cool, but we were excited at Bruce's newfound fame and wanted to congratulate him. He warmly shook our hands and asked if we had tickets to the show that night. When we said no, he then turned to his manager and said, "Mike, hook these cats up." Appel then handed us two tickets in the tenth row for that evening's performance. I don't think I ever received a better gift. The show that night was nearly four hours long. I was physically and emotionally drained. I then wrote a lengthy column for the West Catholic News with the headline reading, "50's Elvis - 60's Beatles - 70's Bruce." In 1997, at our 20th class reunion, I was introduced as the guy that turned the high school on to Bruce Springsteen. While I was proud of that, I also realized the real credit belonged to Mr. G, who lent me a copy of a debut album by a relatively unknown artist during my freshman year.

# 12

## The Secret Kidd

Writing for the school paper was a real blessing. I was given the freedom to write features on my fellow athletes, and also had the chance to write about music, which was quickly becoming my second love, just behind sports. One day early in my senior year Mr. Crewalk asked me if I'd be interested in interviewing a fledgling singer/songwriter named Kenn Kweder, a 1969 graduate of West. I was not familiar with Kweder's music, but I had seen some posters he had put up in the neighborhood and around the city advertising his band "Kenn Kweder and His Secret Kidds."

Kweder grew up at 69th and Chester Avenue, two blocks from McCreesh playground. I jumped at the chance to interview him because I was becoming a huge fan of singer/songwriters. By this time, I was getting into artists like Springsteen, Jackson Browne, Al Stewart, and Graham Parker. I admired the creativity of these musicians. My interview with Kweder was intriguing. He was funny, down-to-earth, and extremely confident. He shared the stories behind some of the songs he had written. We chatted for over an hour, and then he invited me to attend a Secret Kidds show the following week at Drexel University. He suggested I hold off writing my feature until after I saw him perform live. He then offered to drive me back home, since I took public transportation everywhere, and he had a car, and was still living in the neighborhood.

We stopped at a bar called The Tavern. I was three years shy of my 21st birthday, the legal drinking age in Pennsylvania, but here I was knocking back a couple of screwdrivers with my new friend. I soon learned that hanging with Kweder meant bypassing certain rules and regulations. About a week later, I saw my first Secret Kidds show in a small auditorium on the Drexel campus. I was impressed with the quality of the songs, and Kenn's stage presence. My article in the West Catholic News trumpeted the arrival of a creative and talented artist from our high school who had a chance to make it big. Kenn liked the story and a number of my classmates started coming out to shows and became fans. It was the start of a close friendship that has now lasted over 45 years.

During my final two years in Philly before I took off for my radio career, I honestly thought my buddy Kenn was going to sign a deal with a major label. He was opening for acts like J. Geils Band, Cheap Trick, Patti Smith and Devo. In April of 1978, I attended a show at Houston Hall on the University of Pennsylvania campus as Kenn opened for the New York-based punk group The Ramones. While the Secret Kidds rocked out, the Ramones fans in attendance started getting restless. They wanted to see the Ramones and started yelling for Kweder to get off the stage. This did not sit well with the tough inner-city crowd that Kweder had attracted. Before long, fists and beer bottles started flying. Fights spilled over into the bathroom, which became a bloody mess. There was very little security, so it was total mayhem.

Through it all, the Secret Kidds kept playing, never missing a beat. In all my years of attending shows and concerts, that was the only night I feared for my safety. I stayed for one song by the Ramones and then took the 36 trolley car back into Southwest Philly. Later in 1978, music mogul Clive Davis, who at the time was head of Arista Records, rode his limo from New York City to Philly just to see the Secret Kidds at the Hot Club in center city. He was impressed enough to meet with Kenn for drinks after the show. Davis liked what he heard, but told Kenn that he didn't hear a hit single in the set. Kenn didn't want to compromise and write "nonsensical pop songs," as he puts it. That was that. There was never a record deal and Kweder never made the big time, but he has become a legendary troubadour in and around Philly. Nearly every student who has attended the University of Pennsylvania in the past 30 years is familiar with him because of his regular late Tuesday night shows at Smokey Joe's on the Penn campus.

*Singer/Songwriter Kenn Kweder is one of my best friends and my biggest musical influence*

13

## Change of Plans

When it came time to apply for colleges I was limited because of a lack of funds. My dad was now a bartender and my mom was a housewife. There was not a lot of money for higher education. I would be eligible for some financial aid, but there was no way I could go away to college. I would have to continue living at home and commute. Therefore, I applied for every scholarship I could find and only applied to colleges in the Philadelphia area. The Society of Professional Journalists awarded me a $3,000 scholarship which was a Godsend. I used that money to attend Temple University. The daily commute was not an easy one. I didn't have a car, so I took the #36 trolley car to center city, transferred to the Broad Street subway, taking it north to Columbia Avenue. On a good day, it took about an hour, but if the trolleys got backed up, it could take much longer. At Temple, there were very few opportunities for freshmen to get involved in extracurricular activities.

One class on "Communications Theory" featured a professor reading from a dry, humorless text about the role of the media. This was done in a huge auditorium with nearly 300 other freshmen, who were all majoring in Communications or Radio, TV, and Film. This is not what I had in mind. I wanted to be involved and write, broadcast, and get on air experience. I was unsuccessful in my efforts to get plugged in the way I was at West Catholic High. I was never comfortable at Temple.

Frustrated after just one semester, I set up a meeting with the Dean of the Communications Department, and asked if I could transfer some of my scholarship money to the American Academy of Broadcasting (AAB), which was located in downtown Philadelphia. He wasn't crazy about the idea, but he agreed to give me $1500. I secured a student loan to cover the rest of the tuition and enrolled in the next available class at AAB, which would start in October of 1978. I was taking a huge gamble, but I dreaded the thought of making that commute for the next four years only to sit in large auditoriums with hundreds of other students. At AAB, they promised hands-on training. It was a risk worth taking.

# 14

# AAB

As soon as I started classes at the Academy, I knew I made the right move. Our class of 30 students dove right in, getting hands-on training in every aspect of radio. Writing, recording, anchoring, editing, dubbing, disc jockey operations, and producing commercials were all part of the curriculum. Monday through Friday from 8 am to 4 pm our days were filled with these types of activities under the tutelage of Fast Eddie Coyle, a fast talking 26-year-old Top 40 disc jockey who had already worked in several markets. Fast Eddie was the real deal. This was not a professor with a large textbook preaching theory, but instead a young radio veteran, who worked on the air, and knew how to make his students better and get ready for a potential first job. Eddie helped me get rid of my regional Philly accent, and gave me tips on pace and tempo while reading newscasts. He also taught me to be less wordy and more streamlined in my copy, writing for the ear instead of the eye.

Early on, Eddie realized I was taking this very seriously, and he wouldn't hesitate to give me a pointer or two privately. A handful of other students in the class were also very serious. Matt Mangas, John Rizzo, Gary Smith and I were chosen to produce a one hour 'magazine' show called "Showcase". Each Saturday the four of us would convene at the school's studios with an instructor named Debbie Guyton, and we'd put the show together. Music and sports features, comedy bits, and song parodies filled the hour. The master tape of the show was recorded on a large reel to reel and Debbie would then deliver the reel to WIBF in Jenkintown, Pennsylvania, a Philly suburb. The show aired six nights later at midnight.

"Showcase" may have taken up most of my Saturdays for five months, but it was well worth it. Since my resume at that point was pretty sparse, adding call letters like WIBF gave me some credibility. By the way, I've never stepped foot inside WIBF, or Jenkintown for that matter! As our class neared graduation in April of 1979, one of the school's executives, veteran radio deejay and programmer John Roberts, suggested that I send 300 resumes to small market stations around the country and that strategy worked. On a rainy Thursday morning my dad drove me to the post office and couldn't believe I was carrying out this plan. I had researched the addresses of 300 stations from Florida to Alaska and sent resumes to each. Three days later, I had a job offer on the table from a small station in the midwest. One week later, on April 23rd, 1979, I started my career as the News Director at WKXK in Pana, Illinois.

*AAB days with John Rizzo, yours truly, Matt Mangas, and Gary Smith*

# 15

# Culture Shock

Just three days after accepting the position at WKXK, for the princely sum of $150 a week, I found myself on an airplane for the first time ever. My girlfriend Gerry (who would be my wife two months later) gave me $500 to fly to the midwest to get this radio career started. That gift nearly gutted her entire savings. My parents did what they could do to help financially, and I believe my siblings pitched in some as well. Gerry was going to stay behind in Philly while continuing her job in the Financial Aid office at the University of Pennsylvania. Gerry would join me sometime after her brother Steve's wedding in June.

The closest large airport to Pana was in St. Louis, Missouri, about ninety miles to the southwest. After landing in St. Louis, I took a bus to Springfield, Illinois and transferred to another bus that would take me to Pana, population 6,300. As the bus rolled down State Highway 29 between Taylorville and Pana, all I could see was miles and miles of cornfields, interrupted by an occasional meadow where cows grazed. I thought to myself, "Toto, we aren't in Southwest Philly anymore." Shortly after arriving in Pana, the bus driver pulled into a small shopping center and stopped in front of a laundromat, where several passengers, including me, got off.

This town was so small the bus station was also a laundromat! It was late on a Saturday afternoon and there was nobody around. I stood there for a moment with all my worldly possessions which included the suitcase in my hand and about $200 in my wallet. I used a payphone to call John Grego, the program director at the station. While I was waiting for him to pick me up, I couldn't help but think that as the news director at the radio station, how creative will I have to be to find news in a town like this? Then Grego pulled into the parking lot in a 1973 purple Dodge Dart with a white vinyl top. I don't know why, but I'll never forget that car or that moment. My radio career would start here, in this rural town in Central Illinois.

# 16

## A disastrous debut

Even though my main responsibilities as News Director at WKXK were the gathering, writing and reporting of local news, I was also promised a chance to do some play-by-play of area high school games. The station already had a sports director, Jim Keegan, who served as the play-by-play voice of the Pana High School Panthers. Keegan broadcast all the Pana football and basketball games, and was very good at it. The station did not broadcast baseball.

Early in the basketball season, I was offered a chance to do play-by-play of a tournament game featuring two small area high schools, Stewardson/Stasburg and Cowden/Herrick. I was very excited about the opportunity to call this game, but knew absolutely nothing about either team. I can count on one hand the times I was truly nervous during my four decades of radio, but I remember vividly being anxious on this evening. I wanted to prove I could broadcast a game.

I hurriedly wrote down the lineups and made my way to the broadcast location in the top row of the bleachers, where there was a desk set up. Neither team had their school name in the front of their jerseys. It wasn't until the first timeout that my broadcast partner John Grego told me that I had the teams mixed up. My lineups were correct, but the teams were reversed. I was absolutely devastated. This was my first live broadcast of a basketball game and I had screwed it up completely. I'm sure the audience that evening was very small, and after the gaffe was pointed out to me, I soldiered on. However, when the game was over I remember getting visibly upset.

I was afraid I had blown my chance, and wouldn't have any more games to call. Grego was very kind and told me I had bounced back just fine and I'd have more games to work. It was just a week later when another co-worker, Tom Latonis, asked me to broadcast a game featuring the Nokomis Redskins, a high school team that he usually covered. I jumped at the chance, and was assigned a handful of games. I'll always be thankful to Grego and Latonis for letting me get back up on the horse I so desperately wanted to ride.

## 17

## What Blizzard?

After getting that first taste of basketball play-by-play, I knew the only way to get better was to work more games, but how? There were four on-air guys at the station that enjoyed calling games and there just weren't many opportunities. 40 miles east of Pana is Mattoon, Illinois, home of Lakeland Junior College. As a newsman, I covered the school since it was one of the closest institutions of higher learning.

I heard about a class that gave the students a chance to call the Lakeland Junior College men's and women's basketball games. I enrolled in the class, and Mr. Ken Beno assigned me to work six games between January and March. One men's game, between Lakeland and Kankakee, was scheduled on a Friday night at the home gym in Mattoon. I remember recording my afternoon newscast at WKXK so I'd have plenty of time to get to the gym since snow was in the forecast.

Gerry wasn't crazy about the idea of me driving 80 miles round trip with a good chance of snow, and offered to come along for the game. It got dark very early that day, and by the time we headed east on Highway 16 flurries were coming down. About 15 minutes into the drive, the heavy stuff started falling, and the wind was blowing hard. Gerry suggested we turn around and go back to Pana, but there was no way I was going to miss a game I was slated to work. On the outskirts of Mattoon, we nearly had to stop because of poor visibility, but our 1971 Buick Skylark was equal to the task, and we got to the gym with about a half-hour to spare.

When I got to the courtside broadcast location, I was surprised to find another student from the class preparing for the game. He looked at me in amazement and asked, "What are you doing here? Mr. Beno told me to do the game because there was no way you could make it in from Pana." My three-word response was, "Well, I'm here." He kindly stepped aside, and let me begin writing down the lineups. During the first timeout, Mr. Beno arrived and told me he admired my dedication. He later assigned me to work a High School State Championship game at the University of Illinois. A portion of the Lakeland-Kankakee game was used in my broadcast tape and helped me land my next gig.

# 18

## Nuptials after the deadbeat dad

June of 1979 was the month Gerry had planned to come to join me in Illinois. With both of us having been raised Catholic, we were hoping to get married in the Catholic Church, but my parish priest informed me that he couldn't perform the ceremony unless we both took a six-month marriage class. My landlord said he wouldn't allow Gerry to live with me unless we were man and wife so we were in a bit of a quandary. A local Methodist preacher agreed to officiate, but no firm date had yet been set. Then tragedy struck.

On a Thursday evening back in Philly, with Gerry by her side, my mom suffered a cerebral hemorrhage. She was rushed to the hospital and lay in a coma. I flew in the next day to be with my family. We hoped for improvement, but there was no brain activity. Nine days after the seizure, my mom died at the age of 59. I have never felt a sense of loss like that. My mom was always my biggest supporter and fan. In the nine years I played organized baseball I think she missed one home game. She wrote me two letters a week during my first two months in Illinois. She knew I was homesick so she'd fill me in on what was happening, sometimes cutting out articles from the Philly newspapers.

Now with my mom gone, I had to regroup and get on with my life, but things were happening so quickly. The folks back at the radio station told me to take my time, but I knew I had to get back to Pana soon to return to work and to start my life with Gerry. The day after my mom's funeral Gerry and I took the 36 trolley car to Center City Philly to get our marriage license. My brother told me he had a friend named Joe Trafka who would help us when we got to City Hall. Neither one of us knew what was happening, but shortly after Mr. Trafka secured our license, he took us into a courtroom and told us to wait.

There were only about a dozen folks in there. A judge was sternly addressing a man who apparently had fallen behind on his child support payments. The judge said something to the effect of, "I don't care how many different women you've gotten pregnant, you are still responsible." A few moments later, the judge announced to the small gathering, "Okay, we're going to change it up a bit. We're going to have a wedding." Gerry just happened to have our wedding rings in her purse.

Just like that, the judge called me and Gerry up to the front of the courtroom. Mr. Trafka served as a witness, and five minutes later, we were married. Neither one of us had any idea we were getting hitched that day. We were basically just a pair of 20-year-old kids who didn't know what was going on. We really didn't have much of a reception, just pizza and spaghetti with immediate family members at a place called Vince's on Elmwood Avenue. Vince's was right next door the massive General Electric factory, which took up three long city blocks, and was right around the corner from John Bartram High School, Gerry's alma mater, also known as the high school that produced singer Patti LaBelle, Basketball Hall of Famer Earl "the Pearl" Monroe, and

Joe "JellyBean" Bryant, father of the legendary Kobe Bean Bryant.

Gerry, now two years removed from high school graduation, was about to go to a small town in the midwest to be with a guy making $150 a week at a tiny radio station. The following day we flew to Illinois and started our life together. On the date of our second anniversary, Father Pat Hoffman blessed our marriage in the church during a small private ceremony.

---

When my dad passed away in 1988 of a massive heart attack at the age of 70, our family was stunned and saddened. We should not have been totally shocked, however. Bill Schoening Sr. was gregarious and fun-loving, but never really took good care of himself. He had quit smoking but for years he puffed Chesterfields. His decades of gambling, overeating, and drinking into the wee hours finally caught up with him when he collapsed and died after a night at an Atlantic City casino. About a decade later, I sat down with pen in hand to write a tribute.

I wanted to paint an accurate picture but from the perspective of a son who enjoyed his dad's company and cherished the early years of Phillies games and horse races. I still miss my dad, but I'm never sad when I think of him. He lived life to the fullest and usually had a big smile on his face. Surviving a kamikaze attack in the South Pacific just a few months after his younger brother was killed in France had a big impact. Although he was usually upbeat and positive, I think deep down it was hard for him to cope with losing 159 shipmates and his younger brother. Perhaps his drinking was a way to deal with that sense of loss.

### "My Dad's Days"

*Off the coast of Okinawa   It was early '45*

*The kamikazes sunk the Drexler   Somehow the gunner's mate survived*

*Twelve hours in the water changes how you dream*

*Those future winter mornings were colder than they seemed*

*Chorus*

*These are scenes from my dad's days*

*He touched many people in different ways*

*I wish you knew him   I wish he was here*

*A patriotic tune     a shot and a beer*

*Twenty years later we were down the third base line*

*Koufax was pitching   The Phils were behind*

*He told old stories   He loved to look back*

*To the days of Jimmie Foxx and Connie Mack*

*Repeat Chorus*

*In the seventies still driving a '48 car*

*First he was a bread man   then he tended bar*

*His daughters got married and moved away*

*Guess who stole the show on their wedding day?*

*Strike up the band he'd say   Let's give it a whirl*

*Do you guys know the tune "Daddy's Little Girl"?*

*Repeat Chorus*

*The trifecta window   NFL parlay*

*Buck a hand poker   Do you wanna play?*

*The party ended in '88*

*70 years from his starting gate*

*This old neighborhood will never be the same*

*I saw an oldtimer yesterday still speaking his name*

*Repeat Chorus*

Bill Schoening Sr. tending bar at Hastings Cafe

# 19

## Go west young man

By the summer of 1980, I was getting pretty good at anchoring and writing the local news but that's not what I wanted to do. I had worked about 10 basketball games the previous winter, and that wasn't nearly enough. I needed to work more games. Each week when the national publication "Radio and Records" arrived at the station, I quickly perused the section where job openings were posted. In mid-June, I saw an ad that looked like it was written specifically for me. "Do you eat, breathe and sleep sports? Come and pay your dues at KPET in Lamesa, Texas."

I had no idea where Lamesa was, but I got a tape and resume in the mail immediately. About a month later I received a call from Dorothy Haney, the sales manager at KPET. She had a very thick West Texas accent but was warm and friendly. We chatted for a few brief moments, and then she offered me the position of sports director and evening disc jockey. She explained that I would be paid $750 a month, and I would be the play-by-play voice of the Lamesa High Golden Tornadoes for football, basketball, and baseball. I'd get $10 per basketball and baseball game and $25 per game for football. I would also be working the 7 pm to midnight shift spinning country and western records on nights I didn't have a game. I basically accepted the job right away but I wanted to double-check with Gerry.

When we got out an atlas to see Lamesa's geographic location. Gerry remarked, "It looks like this town is in the middle of a desert." My response was "Let's go." Two weeks later, we loaded all of our belongings into our '71 Buick Skylark and headed to West Texas. It may not have been a desert, but it was pretty close. 1980 was a very hot and dry summer in west Texas, where it's pretty much always hot and dry. On Highway 87, somewhere between Lubbock and Lamesa, all we could see was brown. Hot winds blew brown particles of dust everywhere. We stopped in the town of Tahoka to get some gas, and Gerry said to me, "If Lamesa looks anything like Tahoka, we're going back to Philly." I know she said it partly in jest, but she had a point. About a half-hour later we rolled into Lamesa, and I was thinking that this town looks exactly like Tahoka, but four times bigger. Then I saw what may have been my saving grace, as I exclaimed, "Look Gerry this place does NOT look like Tahoka at all. See, there's a Pizza Hut!"

# 20

## I'm a Yankee?

Shortly after arriving in Lamesa, Dorothy (my new boss) asked if I wouldn't mind helping out in the news department. She explained that she wasn't thrilled with the job being done by the news director. She said I could still do all the sports, and wouldn't have to worry about the nighttime C&W air shift. To be honest, I really didn't want the news responsibilities, but Dorothy was convinced I'd be more valuable to the station as a reporter/anchor. Once I agreed, she took me around town and introduced me to the movers and shakers, including the School Board president, the mayor, police chief, and the Dawson County Sheriff, JD Bartlett.

Sheriff Bartlett had a belly and wore a big white cowboy hat and starched shirt. He spoke in a deep, slow West Texas drawl. It's like he was right out of central casting. Picture, if you will, Jackie Gleason's character in the *Cannonball Run* movies. Sheriff Bartlett invited me into his office and asked about my background. When I told him I was born and raised in Philadelphia, he stopped me. "Philadelphia is in Pennsylvania, right? Well, that qualifies you as a blue-bellied Yankee." I responded by telling him New York is where the Yankees were from, but I was a Phillies fan.

Nonplussed, the Sheriff continued, "No, I mean you are from north of the Mason Dixon line. You're a Yankee!" I thought at first he was kidding, but I could see a glaring look in his eyes. I had never been called a Yankee before. My great grandfather, Rudolf Schoening, sailed to the states from Germany in 1882, seventeen years after the conclusion of the Civil War. My family had nothing to do with the Civil War, although that didn't seem to matter to the sheriff. Defending my position seemed to be going nowhere, so I just reminded the sheriff that the Civil War ended in 1865, and this was 1980. I told him, "Sheriff Bartlett, with all due respect, that war ended 115 years ago." His reply was short but telling, "Not for all of us it didn't." Believe it or not, the sheriff and I eventually got along just fine because he liked listening to the Golden Tornadoes on the radio, and I never brought up Ulysses S. Grant or William T. Sherman.

## 21

## The Spanish Mass

One of the best aspects of living in Lamesa was the faith community I encountered at St. Margaret Mary Church. There were only about 25 non-Hispanic families in the entire parish, but Gerry and I were immediately welcomed with open arms, and I was recruited to read scripture while Gerry helped with communion. Gerry and I always attended the Sunday morning service in English, but the most popular Mass was said in Spanish on Saturday nights, and that was no big surprise. Many of these folks were first or second generation from Mexico, and some were understandably more comfortable worshipping in Spanish.

In February of 1982, my dad came down to Lamesa for a visit. Bill Schoening Sr. never missed Mass. No matter how late he was out on Saturday night (and he was out late a lot) and no matter how much he drank (and he drank a lot) he would always go to the 8:15 Mass on Sunday morning at St. Clement's. He usually took his two elderly aunts, Gertrude and Mildred, and then he'd treat them to breakfast at the Llanerch Diner on West Chester Pike. Anyway, I got to thinking about the best way to give my Dad a good West Texas welcome. Knowing that he would not want to miss Church, I suggested we go on Saturday night. He liked the idea of a Saturday night Mass, but I never told him it would be in Spanish. My dad was street smart but not very worldly. When we walked in just prior to the start of Mass, he quickly realized we were the only "gringos" in the entire place.

He looked around in utter amazement and whispered into my ear, "Billy, I've never seen so many Puerto Ricans at one time in my entire life." Then the mariachi band kicked in, and my father, who didn't know a word of Spanish, grabbed a hymnal and tried to sing along. All I remember was a loud off-key version of "Seatu Nombre." As the service went on, he got into it, saying it reminded him of when the Mass was said in Latin before 1962. I eventually informed him that these wonderful folks were Mexican, and not Puerto Rican. After the Mass, I introduced him to my co-worker, Marcelino Hernandez, who hosted a Tejano Show on our FM Station, KCOT. My dad greeted him with a warm handshake, "How ya doin' Mousalito, nice to meet ya." I corrected him and said, "Dad, his name is Marcelino." "That's a little tough for me," was my dad's reply, "I'll just call him Manuel." Marcellino actually got a kick out of all this. He thought he had met the real-life Archie Bunker.

## 22

## "I just want to call Agnes"

The Lamesa High Golden Tornadoes competed in District 2-4A, an athletic conference that stretched from the South Plains to the Permian Basin to the Concho Valley of West Texas. One district foe, Fort Stockton, was 161 miles away. The coaches privately called it "Fort F#ckin' Stockton, because it is 'so f#ckin' far." I couldn't believe we rode three hours one way to play a conference opponent. Back home if we drove three hours south we'd be in Virginia or D.C.

During the 1981 Golden Tor Football season, I was calling an epic battle between Lamesa and the Sweetwater Mustangs, live from the Mustang Bowl. Each team in the school district was responsible for installing a phone line in the visiting radio booth. Little did I know that the line we would use that night would be a multiple-use or "party" line. This is pretty much what happened on the air that night…

BS: "…second down and eight for the Tors from the Sweetwater 42 yard line…"
*LOUD click*
Unknown Lady: "Hello, I need to call my sister Agnes."

BS: "This is Lamesa Golden Tornado football on KPET Lamesa. Pass to the left sideline, intended for Blake McKinney. Incomplete. That brings up a third and eight."
Unknown Lady: "I don't care about football. I just need a line to call Agnes."
BS: "It's Sweetwater 14, Lamesa 7. 4:52 remaining in the second quarter. We are on the air live."
Unknown Lady: "Who cares? Get off my phone!"
BS: "Golden Tornado football on KPET continues in a moment."

At that point, I told the board operator back at the station to disconnect and call right back. It worked. We only missed an unsuccessful third and 8 and a punt. We reconnected, and the unknown lady never returned, at least not that night. To this day, however, whenever I'm on the air and hear any sort of click, I'm expecting to hear a lady on the line trying to call her sister Agnes.

# 23

## Gelding for Sale

In most small-market stations back in the early 80s, on-air talent would come and go. The longer one stayed at a station, the more responsibility one was likely to assume. After one year at KPET, Dorothy put me in charge of finding talent in an effort to stabilize a revolving door situation. Over the next two years, I hired four broadcasters, all from the east coast. I brought in three American Academy of Broadcasting alums including John Rizzo, my best friend from AAB and a very talented on-air personality. I just happened to call him when he was between gigs.

He was a knowledgeable music guy and when he got to KPET he completely revamped and modernized the music filing system. Rizzo knew his time in Lamesa wasn't going to be long-term, but he enjoyed the down-home, laid-back style of west Texas. On Saturday mornings we had a show called "Tell and Sell," and that program featured folks calling the station to announce what they were selling or what they were looking to buy. Old trucks, bed frames, used furniture, car parts, whatever. It was an absolute hoot.

I usually hosted the show but had a remote one Saturday morning, so Rizzo got to host his first "Tell and Sell." He had only arrived at the station a few weeks earlier. One of the first callers was an older woman with a slow, thick West Texas drawl. She told Rizzo and the listening audience that she was looking to sell off her 6-year-old gelding horse. Without hesitation, Rizzo says, "Well ma'am, exactly what makes your horse a gelding?" After a three-second pause, the woman says, "Well, if y'all don't know, I'm not about to tell y'all here on the radio." Welcome to west Texas Rizzo! Just in case you didn't know, a gelding is a horse that's been castrated. Oh, how I wish she would've explained that on the air!

24

## Live from the Janitor's Closet

One January night in 1982 I boarded the yellow dog school bus with the Golden Tor basketball team for that three-hour drive to Fort F#ckin' Stockton. We got to the high school about two hours before game time, but the telephone line at courtside had been shut off. No dial tone. It was after 5 PM so there was nobody at the Fort Stockton office of Southwestern Bell. I tracked down the school custodian and asked him if there was a working phone somewhere close to the basketball court. I was pretty desperate.

On the second floor above the gym, there was a phone in a coach's office. There was no window overlooking the court, but right next door, in the custodian's storage space, there was a window with a view of the court, just behind and to the left of the basket. I found a desk in a classroom across the hall and I was in business. I brought the desk into the closet and set it up next to the window. The board operator at the station called the coach's office. I answered, unscrewed the speaker part of the phone, and fastened alligator clips (I kid you not) which connected to my mixer. I then strung about thirty feet of power cord into my "booth." Amid the brooms, mops, plungers, and washrags, I called a Lamesa road win over Fort Stockton. In over four decades of calling basketball games, that's the only time I ever broadcast a game from a closet.

## 25

## The College Try

By the spring of 1983, I had just completed my third athletic season as the voice of the Lamesa Golden Tornadoes. I was 24 years old, had four years of full-time on-air experience, and was ready for the next step. In mid-June, I got a heads up from former co-worker Chuck Clements, who was working at KSAM Radio in Huntsville, a college town in east Texas, about 70 miles north of Houston. Chuck explained that Sam Houston State play-by-play man Kooter Roberson was leaving KSAM to become Sports Editor of a new daily local newspaper, The Huntsville Morning News.

At that point, I had tapes and resumes ready to go, and got one to KSAM General Manager Ray Eller that day. The following Saturday night, Eller called me and offered me my first college play-by-play job. There would be news responsibilities too, but this was clearly a golden opportunity. At the time, Sam Houston State was in NCAA Division II, members of the Lone Star Conference, featuring opponents such as Southwest Texas, East Texas State, Abilene Christian, Texas A&I, and arch-rival Stephen F. Austin.

At the time I recall thinking how fortunate I had been so far. We found a small apartment close to downtown so Gerry could walk to work, as she landed a job as a teller at Huntsville National Bank. For the next six years KSAM Radio, Huntsville, Sam Houston State, and the Texas Department of Corrections were all important parts of my life.

*From the Booth~Sam Houston State at Boise State*

## 26

# Back to the newsroom

My responsibilities at KSAM included gathering, writing, and reporting local news. In Huntsville that would mean covering the Texas prison system, which is based there. My main three "news beats" were the school district, the University, and the prison system. About two weeks into my tenure at KSAM, Hurricane Alicia ripped through East Texas, causing loss of life and property. It was the first time I had ever covered a major storm. Power was out in some rural areas for weeks.

It presented a challenge, especially since we were still settling in and I was also trying to prepare for my first season calling college football. In the '80s, the death penalty had just been reinstated by the U.S. Supreme Court, and the State of Texas was ready to carry out the orders in Capital Murder convictions. In my six years covering Texas Prisons, I became a regular correspondent for the Texas Associated Press and their Radio Network. AP in Washington was always interested in stories like prison violence, overcrowding, and executions. I was on-site at the prison and covered 29 lethal injections, witnessing a handful.

To this day, people ask me about that experience and are amazed that I was on hand for every execution during a six-year period.

In a conversation with Kooter Roberson (who had returned to KSAM as a morning on-air personality), he asked me how much money the networks were paying me for execution coverage. I hadn't really thought about it too much but estimated it was somewhere around $80. A few weeks later, Kooter happened to be in the AP Wire room at the radio station around 7:45 am when he noticed a story coming across the wire that he knew would be of interest to both me and my listeners.

He told me to turn up the monitor in the newsroom because he had an announcement to make after the next song. He walked back into the control room and turned on his microphone, "That was George Strait on KSAM 1490. We now have breaking news from the Associated Press. James David Autrey, who was scheduled to die at the walls unit tonight by lethal injection, has been granted a stay of execution by the U.S. Circuit Court of Appeals. Bill Schoening will have further details on this story at 8:00 during local news. Again, no execution tonight here in Huntsville. This will cost Schoening about $80."

# 27

# Chatting it up with a serial killer

The public information officer for TDC was a fellow by the name of Charlie Brown, who arranged interviews with inmates on death row. A well-known inmate awaiting execution at the time was Henry Lee Lucas, a drifter who had been convicted in the killing of eleven different people but who had confessed to more than 100 other murders while in prison. For some reason, I thought it might be interesting to interview him. Charlie set it up, but there was a catch. Before Lucas agreed to talk to me, I had to buy him a pack of cigarettes and an orange soda. I think it cost me $1.50.

We were separated by a thick glass window, but there was a small slot, through which I could place my microphone. When he sat down he was pleasant, smiling, and willing to talk about anything. Soon the interview turned into a rambling diatribe that made very little sense. Lucas would mention how he wanted to kill his grandmother when he was a kid, and then in the next breath, he would quote passages from the Book of Corinthians or some other chapter from the New Testament. Lucas also had a "weak eye," as his left eye would look ahead while the right drifted aimlessly. I was always taught to make eye contact during an interview, but I didn't know which eye to look into. I was trying to guess in my mind which was the good eye. I know, awkward.

I tried to reel him in and discuss life on death row, but he continued with his verbal meandering, making very little sense. I politely thanked him for his time, ended the interview and headed back to town. Death Row was located in the Ellis One Unit, about a twenty-minute drive from the radio station. On the way back, I listened to the tape and thought I might be able to salvage a story or two from this conversation if I did some good editing.

Diana Jensen from AP in Dallas called to see if there was anything going on at the prison. I said it was fairly quiet but that I had just returned from a one on one interview with Lucas. Diana explained it was a slow news day, and they could use a package or two. I sent two reports, plus a handful of "actualities," which are short snippets of a subject's voice. About a week later I received a check for $50 from AP for the Lucas stories. After forking out $1.50 for soda and cigarettes, I cleared $48.50 for that 10-minute chat with a disturbed serial killer. In the mid-'80s in small market radio, $48.50 came in handy! Lucas never was executed but died in prison in 2001 at the age of 64.

---

Even though I grew up in the inner city, the neighborhood that immediately surrounded me was all white. My section of Southwest Philly was basically divided by Catholic parishes. Most of the families were second or third generation from the old country with deep roots in Ireland, Italy or Germany. We even had a small Polish Church (St. Mary of Czestochowa.) Since I was a huge sports fan, many of my favorite athletes were black

(Joe Frazier in boxing, Wilt Chamberlain in basketball and Richie Allen in baseball) but I honestly hadn't had an opportunity to get to know any people of color.

That changed at West Catholic High. The diversity of the student population, the creative opportunities encouraged by the faculty, and the nurturing and moral guidance of the Christian Brothers made West Catholic High a very special place for me. Unity and brotherhood were central themes during the turbulent '70s. I wrote "Take Care My Brother" because I truly believe God created us to love one another, regardless of whatever differences we may have. The second verse of this song reflects how I sometimes feel; that the idea of true brotherhood is still elusive, just like that vision in your dream.

---

***"Take Care My Brother"***

*It's like the flowers on a hill   different colors for your eyes*

*They blend together and they will be there on the day I die*

*Chorus*

*Take care my brother  Make sure your faith abounds*

*Always love one another  Black white yellow red and brown*

*It's like the vision in your dream*

*Through the haze you see a light*

*It's moving closer so it seems*

*Then it's fading from your sight*

*Repeat Chorus*

---

*Mike Vasquez and Nic Whitworth have helped shape many of the melodies I've written*

# 28

## "The Voice of Death"

Although I was trying to establish myself as a sportscaster and a play-by-play guy, stations around the state of Texas were more familiar with my news reports. I had become a fairly reliable correspondent for the Associated Press. A program director in Houston called to offer me a news anchor position. The position was in a major market and would pay much more than what I was making in Huntsville, but I was determined that my next career move was going to be in sports.

In 1987, AP named me the winner of the Jordan-Flaherty Award, which goes to the station or news department in the state that is most loyal in filing stories. There was a public fascination with the growing number of lethal injections. I honestly filed those reports because I knew there would be some compensation, but I was having a hard time making larger stations understand that I was a sports guy.

At an awards banquet in Odessa (during which I was presented the Jordan Flaherty award) I was introduced as "The Voice of Death in Texas." The banquet was held in a large ballroom at a hotel. In an adjacent ballroom, a wedding reception was in full swing. As I took the podium to accept my award and say a few words, the band next door loudly broke into their version of "Jailhouse Rock." You can't make this stuff up.

## 29

## High Towering Drive

Late in the summer of 1985, I was playing with one-year-old son Eric at our Huntsville apartment when I got a phone call from my brother Tom in South Philly. He told me that WCAU Radio, the Phillies' flagship station, was conducting a Harry Kalas sound-alike contest. Tom knew I had imitated Harry since he joined the Phillies broadcast team in 1971. He gave me the station number and I tried unsuccessfully to get through for about 15-20 minutes. I was about to give up when I finally got a ring and the producer hurriedly asked my name and told me to have a 20-second impersonation ready to go, as he would put me on live.

The show was hosted by Steve Frederick and the panel of judges included Paul Owens, Phillies General Manager. I got to hear the guy who went on before me and he was absolutely horrible. All of a sudden, I got a boost of confidence. I then heard Frederick say, "Next up is Bill Schoening, who's calling from Texas – let's hear what ya got, Bill." I broke into my signature Harry call, "High towering drive, deep right-center field...Maddox racing under...on his horse and...he squeezes it for out number 2."

Immediately Frederick tells the listening audience that Owens has two thumbs up and Bill Schoening is advancing.

After the show, the producer called to tell me I was one of five finalists for the live contest, which would be held at Veterans Stadium between games of an upcoming Friday twi-night doubleheader. The grand prize was a pair of season tickets for the 1986 season. I had to miss doing color for a high school football broadcast that night, but my brother Tom flew me into Philly so I could give it a shot. I almost returned Tom's investment, but I lost in the finals to a University of Pennsylvania student named Scott Graham. I actually thought I deserved to win but I believe I was hurt by the fact that the scoreboard spelled out all of the contestant's names and hometowns. The listing of "Bill Schoening - Huntsville, Texas" did not help.

The other four contestants were from the area. These folks had no idea that I had been in the stands for many years, right next to them cheering for some bad ballclubs. I was as loyal as they come. However, I accepted defeat that night and shook the hand of winner Scott Graham, and I also got to meet Harry. After the contest, as I was walking toward the runway behind the plate to return to my seat, a well-dressed middle-aged woman approached me. I recognized her as Harry's wife.

She whispered to me that in her opinion I should have won. That was a good moral victory for me. Who knew what Harry sounded like better than his wife? I was given a Phillie's duffel bag and some other "parting gifts." Scott Graham, by the way, has fashioned a very successful sportscasting career for himself. He is now the Voice of NFL Films and has called games for the Phillies, Fox Sports, and Westwood One. I guess if I had to finish second to somebody, it might as well be to a guy who would later narrate for NFL Films!

## 30

## Dizzy Lizzy Strikes

I have always had close relationships with each of my four siblings, and my sister Liz is no exception. Even though she is 12 years older, we have always had a connection. In our family, she is affectionately known as "Dizzy Lizzy." If you're enjoying my stories, you should hear some of hers, one of which includes baking some brownies for an NFL defensive back. Apparently, this player was rude to Liz on multiple occasions so she offered the treat as sort of an olive branch. The only problem was that the brownies were laced with Ex-Lax. That was quite a peace offering, sis.

In the fall of 1988, Liz came down to Huntsville for a visit. I had to work at KSAM one day during her visit, so I invited her to shadow me for the day in my news/sports reporter duties. I had to stop by the Chamber of Commerce to pick up a press release when Liz had an idea. She asked if there was someone at the Chamber that might believe her if she said I was her ex-husband and she was trying to track me down. I immediately thought of receptionist Penny Herzog. I stayed behind a partition while Liz, without any rehearsal, walked into the Chamber of Commerce lobby, desperately looking for clues to find her long-lost ex-husband, me!

She approached Penny, showed her ID with the name Elizabeth Schoening, and then showed her a photo of me from years earlier. Liz then asked Penny if she knew the man in the photo. When Penny confirmed it was indeed Bill Schoening and that I was working at the local radio station, Liz collapsed into the chair next to Penny's desk and started to get very emotional. "After all these years, I can't believe I have finally found him," she cried. Penny got nearly as upset as Liz did, and tried to comfort her, as Liz continued her ridiculous, but apparently believable, story.

The tale included emotional abuse and abandonment of several small children. I waited for a few minutes, and then I walked into the lobby, unaware that the woman I had "abandoned" had finally found me. When Penny saw me enter, the look of shock and horror on her face was so priceless that Liz and I couldn't help it - we both started laughing. I then said, "Hey Penny, I guess you've met my sister. We call her Dizzy Lizzy." At first, I think she wanted to strangle both of us but was a pretty good sport about it. We bumped into Penny later that evening at a local restaurant/bar. I bought her a drink and all was forgiven, but they did recount that story around the Huntsville Chamber of Commerce for quite a few years.

*The Schoening siblings ~ Tom, Chris, Peg, Me, and Liz*

## 31

## Saving the KSAM Car

When Gary Moss was hired as head basketball coach at Sam Houston State in 1987, local car dealer Johnny Holland hosted a welcome party at his beautiful home on the edge of town. I drove the KSAM News car to the party. I had not planned on drinking more than one or two cocktails, but I wanted to be social and get to know the new coach since I'd be working closely with him the following season. For most of the evening, I sat on a barstool, completely oblivious to the fact that one of the bartenders was "topping off" my vodka and orange juice every chance she got. I am NOT blaming the bartender, but I definitely had more vodka than I thought I had.

When it came time to head back into town, one of the star players on the team, a power forward from California named Doug DeVore, asked me if I could drop him off at his apartment. Doug and I said our goodbyes, and we left the party. Johnny's house sits on the edge of a scenic lake, with a concrete boat ramp leading to the water's edge. As I backed out of my spot, I felt the car sliding down the boat ramp. I tried applying the brake, but it was no use. The tail end of the KSAM News car was now partially submerged in Johnny's lake. Doug and I got out of the car, waded through the shallow water, and walked up the ramp.

By now, the entire party had stepped outside to see if the KSAM Car was going to drift into the middle of the lake. These folks should've paid a cover charge since they were enjoying this so much. Never before or since have I witnessed so much laughter at my expense. I was tipsy but sober enough to realize I might lose my job over this.

Assistant Coach Ron Meikle and Johnny quickly moved a farm tractor into place and pulled the car from the lake before it became completely submerged. There were cheers from the crowd, and I was beyond relieved. DeVore decided to go back to his apartment with someone else (imagine that!) Thankfully, the car was still functional but I agreed to let someone else drive me home. The next day I remembered that our remote broadcast unit (called a Norcom) was in the trunk. When I went to retrieve it, the unit was completely waterlogged and not working.

Later that day, I remember seeing our broadcast engineer Doug Mullins trying to blow dry the inside of the unit with a hairdryer. Doug could fix anything. We used that Norcom for the next two seasons, although it never really was quite the same. General Manager Jim Carroll gave me a warning about driving the station vehicle while under the influence, but he never threatened to fire me. On my way out of his office, he said, "Well, at least you have learned a lesson, plus you'll have a story to tell." He was correct on both counts.

## 32

## Montana State 52 Sam Houston State 48

In September of 1987, Sam Houston traveled to Bozeman, Montana for a nonconference game with Montana State of the Big Sky Conference. It was a gorgeous clear day with the scenic backdrop of the Gallatin Mountain Range. There was a ceremony honoring former Montana State star kicker Jan Stenerud before the game. I didn't know it until that day that Stenerud, who hails from Norway, attended Montana State on a ski scholarship. The game that day was wild. Both quarterbacks put up astronomical statistics, and there was over 1,000 yards of total offense amassed by the two teams. The game went back and forth. I was calling the game by myself, but never got tired.

During a timeout late in the third quarter, with Montana State leading 42-41, I made eye contact with Sam Houston State secondary coach Bobby Williams, who was to my left in an adjacent booth. When I said to him, "Wow, what a game!", he flipped me the biggest bird I have ever seen. It was then that I realized the secondary coach of the team that had given up 42 points already probably wasn't enjoying the game as much as I was. Montana State prevailed 52-48 in the highest scoring football game I ever called.

After the game, I got in my rental car and drove south through Paradise Valley and into the northern reaches of Yellowstone National Park in Wyoming. It was the most breathtaking natural scenery I had ever seen. Mountain streams were flowing just a few yards from the side of the road, Majestic peaks, wide sweeping green valleys, and abundant wildlife dotted the landscape. I vowed that one day I would return to Montana. I'm fortunate enough to say that I have been back on a half dozen occasions, and it has become my favorite state to visit, especially Glacier National Park.

*Iceberg Lake at Glacier National Park*

33

## "Quasi/ Pseudo Division I"

I only got to work with Coach Gary Moss for two basketball seasons, and I thoroughly enjoyed it. He was a fun pregame interview, often finding humor in the good and bad aspects of coaching and traveling. During this time, Sam Houston State was in the process of moving up to NCAA Division I. In football, the Bearkats were competing in Division 1-AA, which is now known as FCS, or Football Championship Series.

Since Sam was moving up, but hadn't completely made the leap, my broadcast partner Kooter Roberson called it "Quasi/Pseudo Division I," which was apropos. During the 1987-88 Hoops season, we traveled to Norman, Oklahoma to play the BIG 8 Conference powerhouse Oklahoma Sooners. Their full court, fast-breaking style produced lots of points. They had two players destined for NBA careers, point guard Mookie Blaylock and forward Stacey King.

Sam Houston State, like many other "quasi Division I schools," played road nonconference games for "guarantees," a sizable check written to the underdog team to help fund their program. The game in Norman, for instance, netted the Sam Houston State athletic coffers the total of a guaranteed $15,000. During my pregame interview, Coach Moss was realistic about the situation. I asked him directly, "Does your team have any chance in this game?" Coach Moss smiled and said, "No, not really, but there are 15,000 reasons we are here." By the way, Oklahoma won 101-69. Oklahoma went on the NCAA Final Four that season, losing to fellow Big 8 member Kansas in the championship game.

# 34

# George

After Jim Carroll left KSAM, George Franz became the new General Manager. George was one of the co-owners of the station and was a pleasant enough fellow, but he was a bit of a spendthrift. With Sam Houston State moving up to NCAA Division I, George would look at the football schedule and cringe, because he knew he would have to pay for my travel. When he looked at the 1988 Football schedule for the first time, he called me into the office and bellowed, "Boise State, really? Why are the Bearkats playing at Boise State? That's in Ida-f#ckin'-ho! I'm going to have to pay for your airfare, hotel, rental car, and meals. Why don't they just play TSU? (TSU is Texas Southern University, located in Houston.) That would be a cheap trip. But no, I gotta send your butt to Ida-f#ckin' ho!"

That basketball season, George decided to not send me on the road for some nonconference games, and instead got a "feed" from the opposing broadcasters. We would simply carry the other team's broadcast. Although it saved some money, our sponsors started complaining when the announcers mispronounced names or talked very little about Sam Houston State. One of the sponsors who complained was local car dealer

Johnny Holland. The following season, which turned out to be my last, I traveled to every game.

George Franz was an admirer of my work but didn't want me to pursue any outside opportunities. During the 1987 football season, television producer Murphy Brown of Home Sports Entertainment in Houston offered me the chance to call the Sam Houston State vs. Stephen F. Austin game on television. Not only was the game going to be telecast across the region, but it also paid $500. That was big money for a small market radio guy in 1987. George refused to excuse me from the radio broadcast, even though my broadcast partner Kooter was more than capable of handling those duties.

I said to myself that the next time a chance like this surfaced, I was going to tell George I was taking it, and not ask for his permission. From time to time, George would give me tips on news stories. One time in the spring of 1988 he told me I should do a story on some medical breakthroughs taking place at Huntsville Memorial Hospital. He informed me that there was a doctor at our local hospital performing three coronary operations a day. I had a hard time believing a doctor could pull that off. He handed me the doctor's card and told me to follow up. This sounded like a great story, although I was somewhat skeptical. Three heart operations in one day? I called and discovered he was an eye doctor. He was performing CORNEA operations, not coronaries!

Another time, George filled me in on a new contest the station would be running in conjunction with the opening of a local shopping mall. "This is going to be a huge promotion," he told me. "Not only do we have an excellent grand prize, we have very good constellation prizes!" I guess we were giving away the moon and the stars!

## 35

## The Pig at Howard Payne

When the Huntsville Morning News folded after only one year of operation, Kooter Roberson came back to KSAM as the morning man, play-by-play for Huntsville High, and color analyst for Sam Houston State football. For the next five years, we traveled by car all over the states of Texas and Louisiana.

Clyde Norris Roberson was given the nickname "Kooter" at a young age. While attending Huntsville High, he started working at the radio station and was an important part of the station for nearly 50 years. I enjoyed traveling with him because he insisted on driving and he knew every alternative road. His knowledge of State Highways and Farm to Market roads was uncanny. He didn't like Interstate Highways and always preferred to take "the circuitous route."

I learned lots of Texas history and geography from him. If we were not in a big hurry, he would stop at historical markers. He prided himself on knowing small towns and obscure facts about Texas. One of my favorite trips with Kooter came in 1984 when both the Sam Houston State Baseball and Softball teams qualified for the NCAA Division II Regionals to be played in South Dakota. The baseball team would be playing in Brookings and the softball team was scheduled to play in Sioux Falls, 57 miles to the south. Both teams lost their first two games and were quickly eliminated. We were finished by 1 pm Saturday.

Since our return flight to Houston wasn't scheduled until Monday morning, we decided not to rush back, and see as much of South Dakota, Nebraska, Iowa and Minnesota as we could. With Kooter doing most of the driving, we put nearly 1,100 miles on the rental car. It's a good thing we had unlimited mileage. I was excited to knock off some states that I hadn't seen before since I had always wanted to see if I could hit all 50 states.

Another of my favorite Kooter stories happened one Saturday night in Brownwood, Texas before a Lone State Conference basketball game at Howard Payne University. Sam Houston Head Coach Robert McPherson noticed some students trying to drum up interest in "Agriculture Night." The students had brought some small pigs courtside to show off to the crowd. The players on both teams had just begun warm-ups, and I was about five minutes away from starting my 15-minute pregame show. Coach McPherson approached Kooter and offered him $20 if he would kiss one of those little pigs. He quickly said no, but I saw my chance to make a quick $20. At the time, I was getting paid $25 per game. I could almost double that in a heartbeat!

I walked out to the court and told Coach McPherson I would kiss one of those pigs, but I'd have to see the money first. Coach pulled out a twenty, showed it to me, and without hesitation, I walked out to midcourt and smacked a big smooch right on the snout of a little pig. As I walked back to my courtside broadcast location, Coach McPherson couldn't believe it. He stood in open-eyed amazement, apparently not believing I went through with it. He looked as if he had just been hit with a technical foul. He turned in my direction and angrily flung that $20 bill onto the table in front of me. I scooped it up quickly, put it in my pocket and started my pregame show.

After Sam Houston's 77-69 win, none of the players would talk to me, several of them avoiding me completely. I didn't understand why. I always got along great with the players. Well, it seems Kooter told the guys I had French kissed the pig for the cash. I think I would've needed at least $50 for that! I sent the details of that story to the Sporting News, a weekly national publication. A few days later, I got a call from Sporting News executive news editor Bob McCoy asking me for further details. In the next edition of the Sporting News, there was a black and white illustration of me kissing the pig, with the little animal looking up at me and saying, "Don't even try to French kiss me, bud, I hardly know you."

# 36

## Early Worm

During the 1984-85 basketball season, Sam Houston State was still in NCAA Division II, and that season the Bearkats were invited to play in the annual Thanksgiving Tournament at Midwestern State University in Wichita Falls, Texas. The host school Midwestern State would be joined by Sam Houston State, The Colorado School of Mines, and the Savages of Southeastern Oklahoma State. That's right, the Savages.

I don't remember much about that weekend, but I clearly recall a gangly 6'8 forward from Southeastern Oklahoma who couldn't shoot but ran the floor, took charges, blocked shots, and grabbed seemingly every rebound available. His only points came off offensive rebounds, and he finished with something like 16 points, 22 rebounds and 6 blocked shots. He had no tattoos and no piercings, at least not yet. His name was Dennis Rodman.

---

When I was a teenager my friend Kenn Kweder introduced me to the music of a very obscure but talented West Philly singer/songwriter named Billy Schied. I only got to see him perform one time, in the winter of 1978 at a bar on Woodland Avenue in Southwest Philly. I was familiar with some of his songs, because Kenn would play them as cover tunes during his unplugged acoustic sets. Schied's tunes were clever lyrically and very melodic. The only thing I remember about that night on Woodland Avenue was that Schied was really good early in the set, but the alcohol consumption started to creep into the quality of the performance. I knew he had the reputation of a hard drinker.

I remember feeling bad for the guy because he had a special talent. My favorite original by Billy Schied was a little ditty called "Back By Noon," but there was only one verse and one chorus. He never completed the tune, and never recorded it. After he passed away in the 1980's, due to cirrhosis of the liver, I encouraged Kweder to finish writing the song, but he never did. I then decided to write a second verse myself, pick up the tempo, and record my own version. Since Billy Schied wrote the original melody for "Back by Noon" in the mid 70s, it was 43 years between the time he started the song and I finished it.

---

**"Back By Noon"**

*I was dancing lightly through life at a furious pace*

*I woke up one morning and had to laugh at my face*

*My eyes were lit up like an old racehorse My hair was imperial blue*

*As I looked at the walls around me I knew exactly what had to do*

*Chorus*

*I went down to my place of business*

*I took all the money out of the safe*

*I locked the doors and closed the windows*
*And hung up a sign with a piece of tape*
*There's a time to die and a time to fly*
*And they both are coming soon*
*If I don't die and I can't fly   I'll be back   back by noon*

*I've been thinking lately it's time for a cool change*
*Staying 'round here is doing me no good*
*If I need a reason there's the change of seasons*
*I'm taking off like I said I would*

*Repeat Chorus*

# 37

## "I'm Here All Week"

Huntsville wasn't known for its plethora of fine dining establishments, but there was a good steakhouse in town called Steak and Spirits. The restaurant had a good reputation and opened up a small nightclub adjacent to the main facility called the S&S Club. The club catered to an older crowd and featured occasional live music. Club Manager Scott Cherryholmes had the idea to bring in live comedy acts once a month. Houston's Bill Hicks was probably the biggest name to play that room. Hicks went on to be featured in HBO Specials and made an international name for himself before dying of cancer at the age of 32.

In 1988, Cherryholmes approached me about hosting an amateur night. I not only got to emcee but I also was given a 10-minute time slot. I will be the first to admit, stand up comedy was scary, but making people laugh was almost intoxicating. I was a little nervous, but many of the folks in the audience knew who I was, so I just kept it local. I didn't really tell jokes; I just told stories and interacted with the crowd. The ten minutes went quickly. One of the stories required the use of an "F" bomb. I remember how liberating it felt to be able to curse into a microphone and not expect to get a phone call or a letter from the FCC. Whenever Cherryholmes needed an emcee, he called me. I think my rate was $50 and a couple of drink tickets.

# 38

## The break I needed

By the dawning of 1989, I had my ears and eyes open for a better opportunity. I loved Huntsville and had made some very good friends there, but I had just turned 30 and was still doing news and working in a small market station. I felt ready for a move up. One Monday morning in early March I got a call from Alan Jones, an assistant Athletic Director at Texas A&M. Jones explained to me that he had listened to a basketball broadcast that previous Saturday between Sam Houston State and Southwest Texas (now Texas State). He told me he liked my work and then asked if I had a baseball tape.

KSAM did not broadcast baseball until the postseason, but I had saved a tape from Sam Houston's 1987 trip to a regional in Austin. Jones then told me that his radio announcer for baseball was leaving to take a TV job in Little Rock. He said he had the road games covered, but needed someone to call home games for the rest of the season. At the time, A&M was the number one team in the country. Their star player was shortstop Chuck Knoblauch, who went on to have a successful major league career playing second base for the Minnesota Twins and New

York Yankees. When Jones offered me the chance to call Aggie baseball, I said yes immediately.

I didn't consult with my boss George Franz, remembering that two years previously he had rejected my request to work a football game on TV. When I returned to the station, I simply informed George that I was doing Aggie baseball on the side for the next couple of months and that I would pay my intern Kelly Bostrom (a very sharp and capable young reporter) out of my own pocket. Kelly would cover meetings or news events that I couldn't. He wasn't fond of the idea, but I reminded him that it was only for the duration of the college baseball season.

It may have been the best move I ever made. The Aggies won the Southwest Conference tournament, hosted a regional, and came within one game of the college world series. They were beaten in the regional final by LSU and future major league pitcher Ben McDonald. Although the Aggies didn't make it to Omaha, I was feeling buoyed and confident. I had gained invaluable experience and had met a few influential folks that might be good contacts down the line. I also got a taste of big-time college sports and was eager for more.

The break I needed • 103

*Calling Texas A&M baseball*

# 39

## LBJ calling

A few weeks later I was on vacation at the Jersey Shore when I got a call from KSAM Program Director Michael Anthony. He said Tom Dore from KLBJ in Austin was trying to track me down. I had met Tom during the A&M vs. Texas baseball series and again at the SWC tournament. Tom had an opening on his sports staff at KLBJ and personally called me, asking me to apply. He also explained to me that he was required to advertise the position, which meant it would take a while to go through all of the tapes he would be receiving.

I had just updated my resume and tape to include A&M baseball. Tom needed someone to broadcast Longhorn baseball, anchor sportscasts in the morning, and host his nightly sports talk show while he traveled with Longhorn football and basketball. In early July, he invited me to Austin to talk about the position and interview for the job at River Place Country Club, while we played a round of golf. The course is extremely tough and has a reputation for being unfair. I think I shot a 103. That was okay though since Tom shot a 105. Two weeks later, on July 14th, 1989 Tom Dore offered me the job.

He told me I beat out 64 other candidates. I'll never forget that day. It had taken me ten years, but I was finally going to work sports full-time and was moving to the coolest city in the state and one of the best cities in the country. I remember crying tears of joy and thanking the Good Lord. I had prayed for an opportunity like this one, and here it was. I was about to go to work for Lady Bird Johnson!

## 40

## Sportstalk with BS

I was in Austin for just a couple of weeks when Sports Director Tom Dore left for KCMO in Kansas City. KLBJ management considered hiring a new sports director and keeping me as the number two guy, but during this time I was working lots of hours and loving every minute of it. Since we hadn't yet hired a replacement for Tom, I was anchoring morning and afternoon drive sports, hosting the evening sports talk show, and attending daily football practice and press briefings for Longhorn football.

Program Director Mark Caesar called me into his office to let me know they were moving me up to sports director and hiring Ed Clements from KCRS in Midland to be my assistant. The good news for me was that I would now be part of the Longhorn Network Coverage and the evening talk show was all mine. I'd also be the analyst and backup play-by-play guy for Longhorn basketball and the main play-by-play voice for Longhorn baseball. Management gave me free rein on my talk show, and I got to work immediately lining up guests.

Tom had left behind a rolodex (remember those?) with hundreds of names and phone numbers. Over the next several years, my guests were virtually a "who's who" of the sports world. Bum

Phillips, Arthur Ashe, Ernie Banks, and Nolan Ryan, just to name a few. In-studio guests included Franco Harris, Ben Crenshaw, Tom Kite, Don Baylor, Archie Griffin, Tom Landry, and Angelo Dundee. Even though play-by-play has always been my first love, I truly enjoyed hosting Sportstalk because I got a chance to pick the brains of many athletes and coaches who had risen to the top of their professions.

I also was able to track down 80-year-old Byrum Saam, who was living in suburban Philadelphia. Although he was battling memory loss and was a bit hard of hearing, he agreed to come on the show. I felt a sense of closure when I told him on the air that his melodic delivery inspired a kid in the summer of 1969 to become a play-by-play guy. I could tell he was touched by the comment, and that meant the world to me. His health slowly declined after that and he died five years later. Ironically, Byrum Saam was a native Texan who spent most of his career in Philadelphia (as the voice of the A's and the Phillies) and I'm a Philly native who has spent most of his career in the state of Texas.

*Penn State and Pittsburgh Steeler running back Franco Harris was one of many cool guests to join me on KLBJ*

## 41

## Spitfire Boss

The General Manager of KLBJ AM and FM in the '80s and early '90s was E.A.W. "Ted" Smith, a feisty native of Britain who had served in the Royal Air Force and fought against the Luftwaffe during WWII. Ted had moved to the States shortly after the war and his radio career ascended through the sales side of the business. His stately accent and proper diction endeared him to several Austin businesses, and they paid Ted to voice their commercials.

As a G.M., he ruled with an iron fist and regularly authored memos which were hung up in several prominent locations around the station. These "missives" were sometimes critical of our performance as a station, telling us all to button down and pay more attention to detail, etc. My favorite memo blasted the male members of the on-air staff for the untidy condition of the men's room. Ted usually used his own private restroom upstairs, but needed to use the restroom downstairs one day. He didn't like what he saw.

I can recall my favorite part of his diatribe word for word, "Upon using the men's lavatory outside the studios today I was utterly appalled. Various periodicals were strewn throughout the facility. Be forewarned: From here on out you shall bring your own dime-store novel to the bloody bogs!" Of course, we all had to look up "bogs," which is a British colloquial expression for toilet. I figured if I didn't have to consult the dictionary at least once, it wasn't a true Ted Smith memo.

Ted was a good boss because he let me do my job. I can't recall one time he was critical of my work or even offered constructive criticism. Honestly, we had very little interaction. When he announced his retirement from the station in 1992, I was out of town. Upon returning to Austin, I called him at his home one to thank him for the opportunity and congratulate him on his retirement. "I thank you too, Bill," he said, "I believe you have made tremendous progress under my personal tutelage." Personal tutelage? Whatever you say, Mr. Smith!

I invited Ted to play golf a few times in the '90s after he retired. He was always pleasant and loved reminiscing. I enjoyed his stories about flying with the RAF over Holland late in the war. He liked the fact that I was interested in the war. He gave me a signed copy of his book "Spitfire Diary," during which he recalled his days as a pilot fighting against the Luftwaffe. We stayed in touch through the years until he passed away in 2012 at the age of 89. When I think about it now, maybe I actually did make some progress under his personal tutelage.

## Coach Gus

By the time I arrived on the scene to cover Longhorn baseball, Coach Cliff Gustafson was already a legend. He had been running one of the nation's most consistent programs for 23 years, including national championships in 1975 and 1983. The Horns qualified for the College World Series in Nebraska so often that they sold burnt orange t-shirts that read, "The University of Texas at Omaha." One bright autumn day, I stopped by fall baseball practice to see how the new prospects were looking for the following spring.

Among the freshmen, I wanted to see a right-handed pitcher from Alvin, Texas named Reid Ryan, son of the legendary pitcher Nolan Ryan. Coach Gus was sitting in a folding chair just outside the dugout. He told me to grab a chair and waved me over. Ryan was pitching in the scrimmage. We watched the freshman warm-up and then face a couple of batters. He had a smooth motion and very good mechanics. He struck out the first batter with a changeup. The next batter lined a fastball up the middle for a base hit. As the third batter was coming to the plate, I commented to Gus that the Ryan kid looked like he had a good changeup and curveball.

The veteran coach looked at me, took a swig of iced tea from a mason jar, and said, "Yeah, but he's got his mama's fastball." A few years later, Texas was playing a Saturday doubleheader in Houston against the Rice Owls. Rice featured a powerful switch hitter named Lance Berkman, who at one time expressed a desire to play at Texas, but instead went to Rice and then wore out the Longhorns for the next three seasons. He went on to be named National College Player of the Year, and has been inducted into the college baseball hall of fame. He also had a successful major league career and was a 6 time all star.

On this sunny day in Houston, Berkman drove in three runs in a 5-4 Rice win. On the bus going back to the hotel, Coach Gus looked very despondent. It looked like the legendary coach needed a boost. I had just started guitar lessons and had my acoustic Ibanez in my room at the hotel. I knew Coach Gus liked to pick and sing a little bit, so I asked him if he wanted to borrow my guitar. He liked the idea and told me to come to his room.

When I knocked on his door he was still wearing his uniform, complete with stirrups on his socks. He had perked up a little bit, but I'm sure the loss of that game was difficult to swallow. I handed him the guitar and he tuned it to his liking. He then sat up in his chair, and said, "Billy, this is a song written by my friend Willie Nelson and made famous by the late Patsy Cline." He then started to strum lightly and sing lowly, "Crazy…I'm crazy for coaching this ballclub…"

# Coach Gus • 113

*In the dugout with legendary Longhorn baseball coach Cliff Gustafson*

# 43

## "Who's on third?"

During my first few years of broadcasting Longhorn baseball, I had several different partners in the booth. Longtime UT Sports Information Director Bill Little worked most of the games with me, and Ed Clements from KLBJ did a handful of games as well. Ed was a jovial, fun-loving, politically incorrect broadcast veteran. When he was the play-by-play voice at Midland Junior College a few years earlier, the basketball players affectionately called him "Mr. Radio."

Having grown up in Brownwood, Ed didn't really have too much exposure to Italian names or any European names for that matter. In the early '90s, Ed was in the booth with me for a home series against Rice. The Owls had a third baseman named Antonio Di Jesualdo (pronounced dee ja SWAL do). As we were writing down the lineups, Ed asked me a couple of times how to pronounce it. I slowly and patiently sounded it out for him. He really wouldn't have to worry about it until the middle three innings when he was scheduled to switch over to play-by-play. As the color analyst, Ed was able to avoid saying the 3rd baseman's name.

In the bottom of the fourth, he was setting the Rice defense, and was okay until he got to the third baseman, whose name apparently was now pronounced, "Did ya swallow?" He tried to correct himself but got himself in deeper. "Again, up on the grass at third is …Did ya swallow?" He said it again! As soon as he said it the first time I looked away because I was trying to suppress my laughter. Ed's face turned crimson red, and he couldn't stop giggling. It was his inning to do play-by-play, and I was not about to save him- he was on this island alone. Once he regained his composure he was fine, but for the rest of the game, the Rice third baseman was known simply as "Antonio."

Ed co-hosted my show whenever we had a remote broadcast, usually live at a bar, restaurant, or other business. One day in 1992 a local company named Pool Pro thought it would be a good idea for us to broadcast from one of their hot tubs. When we got there we found out that the gorgeous Budweiser Girls (three of them) would be donning their sexy swimsuits and joining us in the hot tub for the entire broadcast. One of our callers asked me during the show if I was concerned about getting electrocuted since we were in the water with live microphones. My response was, "Well if I'm going to die, this would be a pretty good way to go."

*Hosting my talk show in a hot tub with the Budweiser Girls. Tough Gig!*

## 44

## "..and now a High Mass..."

Another gentleman with whom I spent a lot of time in the baseball booth was the longtime Sports Information Director at UT, Bill Little, who worked at least a few games (often many) for fifty seasons - from 1967 to 2017. He had already written a book on the history of the Longhorn baseball program and was a walking encyclopedia when it came to Longhorn sports. We were broadcasting a game from Ferrell Field in Waco in 1992 when we noticed students from the Baylor campus station setting up a marti unit just outside our booth.

A marti was a remote transmitter used to send a direct signal from the ballpark back to the station. I had used one for home games back in Lamesa and Pana, but hadn't seen one in a while. Marti units were usually very reliable but once in a while would pick up transmissions from other stations. As we were about to begin the top of the 4th, I handed it off to Bill for the middle three innings. Just as the first batter came to the plate, we heard loud organ music in our headphones. It sounded like a large pipe organ from a church. Then we heard a deep-voiced broadcaster announce that the high mass from St. Louis Cathedral in New Orleans was about to begin.

Bill was trying to describe the baseball game, but in our headphones, we were now hearing a choir singing in French. Apparently, the religious service was not bleeding through on the air, but our concentration was divided between calling the game and figuring out why we were being blessed with an evening Mass from the French Quarter in our headphones.

I finally surmised that it was the marti unit just outside our booth that was causing the issue. Before the bottom of the fourth, I asked the students if they could move their unit a bit further away from us, and that seemed to do the trick, but for one-half inning, we were trying to describe pop-ups and strikeouts while hearing a pipe organ, a priest, and a choir all serenading us in French. Tres Bien!

## Oh...Hi Lesley

The Texas Longhorn men's basketball team had a solid season in '91-92. The SWC regular-season champs had lost to Houston in the conference tournament finals but earned the 8th seed in the Big Dance. The Runnin' Horns were in Greensboro, North Carolina for a first-round matchup with the 9th seeded Iowa Hawkeyes. The day before the game, teams had been assigned practice times at the Greensboro Coliseum.

CBS TV reporter Lesley Visser approached me at the Longhorn practice, introduced herself, and then asked for a few interesting sidebar notes that she might be able to add to her broadcast. I kidded with her saying I would gladly share a little nugget or two if she would stop by for a visit on my talk show, which I would be hosting courtside starting at 7 pm eastern. Duke, the top seed and eventual national champion, was scheduled to practice that night, and nearly 10,000 fans came out to watch.

It was during the Duke practice that Lesley walked by and signaled to me that she would be able to come on for a few minutes. During the next commercial break, as Lesley was putting on her headphones for the interview, I asked Kent Koen, my young producer back in Austin, if he was familiar with her.

Kent had no idea that Lesley was sitting next to me with headphones on, ready to go on the air. "Oh yeah," Kent exclaimed, "she's hot. Man, I REALLY Like her." Without skipping a beat, Lesley responded "Hi Kent!" I don't think I'd ever sensed someone blush from 1300 miles away, but I did that night. Stammering for a moment, Kent managed a very meek, "oh…eh…oh…Hi Leslie." Kent Koen and I worked together at two different radio stations and the Longhorn Radio Network. I have never let him forget the Lesley Visser story. I have crossed paths with Lesley several times after that and I always remind her of "….oh...hi Lesley!"

---

I usually try to let people know I am a Christian through my actions, and not because I get a megaphone and scream it out loud. Two of the central themes of Christianity are to love one another and to not judge others. Those guidelines sound simple, but it's not always easy.

"Ocean Floor" was written to remind myself of God's mercy. I wrote this in the second person, but it could easily apply to me. There have been times in my life when I needed to heavily rely on my faith, and the good Lord was there every time.

---

### *"Ocean Floor"*

*It's an old familiar story perhaps you've heard before*

*About a wrong place and wrong time kind of man*

*He was hot the world was cold or the other way around*

*He was lost more than he was found*

*Chorus*

*He cried out loud   he had his doubts*
*He thought nobody cared anymore*
*He prayed for redemption mercy and love*
*His sins were cast to the ocean floor*
*His sins were cast to the ocean floor*

*At least once in every lifetime you reach a point like this*
*A leap of faith   it's time to sink or swim*
*Status Quo no longer   find out what you've missed*
*Get out of the boat and reach for Him*
*Repeat Chorus*
*The moral of the story is focus when you pray*
*A heartfelt prayer is music to the Lord*
*There's blessing and healing and tears to wipe away*
*And angels who will open up the door*
*Repeat Chorus*

---

## 46

## "How Can a Guy?"

From the time I could pick up WGN Television and the Chicago Cubs games on cable, I liked to imitate Harry Caray. The flamboyant, colorful and sometimes inebriated play-by-play voice of the Cubs was not always accurate or politically correct, but he was consistently entertaining. At some point, a friend told me that Harry couldn't believe catcher Hector Villanueva dropped a pop up after losing track of it, apparently blinded by the sun.

Legend has it that Harry bellowed on air, "How can a guy from Mexico lose the ball in the sun? It's not like the sun doesn't shine down there 365 days a year!" Whether Harry actually uttered those words became irrelevant. It became the staple of my impersonation. From time to time I would entertain players on the Longhorn baseball team with my Harry Caray impersonation. Outfielder Steve Larkin always seemed to enjoy it.

Larkin was the younger brother of Hall of Fame shortstop Barry Larkin, who starred for the Cincinnati Reds. During a nationally televised night game in 1993 at the College World Series, a fly ball was hit deep to left, and Larkin retreated to the warning track, but momentarily lost track of the ball in the lights at

Rosenblatt Stadium. Just before the ball was about to drop, Larkin quickly recovered and was able to snare the fly ball. After the game, I was kidding with Larkin about that play (and his miraculous recovery). He then told me that in that brief moment of panic, all he could think of was Bill Schoening in the booth saying, "How can a guy from Cincinnati lose the ball in the lights?"

21 years later, in August of 2014, I was invited to sit on a Play-by-Play panel at the annual convention hosted by the Texas Association of Broadcasters. I was joined by longtime Baylor University voice John Morris and retired baseball Hall of Fame broadcaster Milo Hamilton, who was well known as the radio voice of the Houston Astros. Hamilton worked alongside Caray when they were both with the Chicago Cubs in the early '80s. It was well known in industry circles that Hamilton and Caray never got along. Apparently there was a huge clash of egos between the two. In his 2006 autobiography, Hamilton referred to Caray as a "miserable human being." At the broadcasters convention Hamilton, Morris and I each gave an opening statement about our career paths. We then opened it up for questions from the audience, which consisted mostly of radio broadcasters and college students who were interested in the field. The first question came from a student in the back of the room. "I have a question for Mr. Hamilton. What was it like to work with the legendary Harry Caray"? At that moment I almost laughed out loud, knowing a bit of the history of their icy relationship. It was all I could do to suppress my laughter. Hamilton was not pleased with the question. He quickly blurted out, "Read the book, kid!"

## "Call Me Chi Chi"

In 1992, Ed Clements and I co-hosted a remote broadcast of "Sportstalk" from the Hula Hut in Austin, where the Celebrity Golf Association was hosting their private pre-tournament party. Ed, who was great at working the crowd, rounded up a number of guests, including Atlanta Falcons quarterback Steve Bartkowski, Chicago Cubs legend Ernie Banks and San Antonio Spurs center David Robinson. (At the time I never dreamed I'd get the chance to call the last two seasons of David's Hall of Fame career.)

With about 15 minutes left in the show, Ed proudly walks up with Johnny Bench, the three-time National League MVP and one of the best catchers in major league history. Wow, I had so many questions for Johnny. As he was sitting down to put the headphones on, I was thinking I would inquire about the '75 World Series, The Big Red Machine, Sparky Anderson, Pete Rose, etc.

As I introduced him on air, Johnny interrupted me, and in a bad Puerto Rican accent, told me to call him by his "real" name- Chi Chi Rodriguez. It was at this point that I realized perhaps Mr. Bench had consumed an adult beverage or two, but I figured he was just joking, so I went back to asking a Cincinnati Reds-related question. Once again, Bench insisted that he was Chi-Chi. I played along and asked him a golf question. After a rambling two minutes of a bad Chi Chi Rodriguez impersonation, I pitched to a commercial, and Johnny (as Chi Chi) thanked me for having him on, never breaking character.

## The real Chi Chi

It is said the PGA Champions Tour (originally called the senior tour) had its origins at the Onion Creek Country Club in Austin during the "Legends of Golf" tournament. Some of the biggest names of golf from the '50s and '60s played every year. I got to meet and interview folks like Arnold Palmer, Lee Trevino, Billy Casper, Don January, and Chi Chi Rodriguez. (The real Chi Chi!)

The tournament, which had moved to Barton Creek Country Club, was unique in format. The field was comprised of two-man teams. One year I decided to follow Chi Chi and his partner Mike Hill for a few holes. I watched as Chi Chi hit a three wood in an attempt to reach a Par 5 on his second shot. The ball was earmarked for a greenside bunker when it took a strange bounce and landed on the collar of the green, and then rolled ten feet from the flag.

After the round, I asked Chi Chi about his approach shot on that hole. "I'll tell you what happened, I hit the "sheet" out of a three wood, but the ball landed next to the bunker near the green. It hit a rake and then bounced up onto the green and rolled close to the hole. The first thing I did when I got up there to the green was move that rake. I did not want that to happen to anybody else."

# 49

## "The hardest working man in show business"

I first crossed paths with Craig Way in the late '80s when he was working on the University of North Texas broadcasts. When I began my work on the Longhorn Network a few years later, Craig was the studio anchor and a very good one. In 1992, when UT and Host Communications made the decision to move me up to the play-by-play seat for football and basketball, Craig went from the studio to the broadcast booth and became my analyst. We hit it off immediately.

Since his background was rooted in play-by-play, he understood the importance of allowing me to finish before he chimed in. He was never too anxious to make a point, but consistently made pertinent observations and did it in a clear, concise manner that made the broadcast go smoothly. In the decade we worked together, we "stepped on each other" only a handful of times. He was prepared and eager to help enhance the broadcast in any way he could.

Craig was already making quite a name for himself in the world of Texas High School Football. He hosted a statewide television scoreboard show on Friday nights and was broadcasting high school games for KRLD in Dallas. He also hosted a weekly syndicated program that showcased high school athletics from every region of the state.

Since he got to travel the back roads on his way to these various high school outposts, Craig became an expert on the geographic regions and farm-to-market roads of the Lone Star state. He also has a photographic memory. If any date makes its way into the brain of Craig Way, there it stays. One day in the mid 90's when Craig was still at KRLD, he gave me a call on my cell phone. I was driving to College Station for a baseball series, and had decided to take a shortcut. Here's the way this conversation went...

BS- Hello.
CW- Hey, where are you?
BS- Hey there, right now I'm driving on Farm to Market Road 696
CW- Oh, have you gotten to Blue or Gus yet?
BS- Blue or Gus?
CW- Well, I assume you're taking a shortcut on your way to College Station and those two towns are on that road.

There was no way he would've had time to look up FM 696, and it's not like Blue and Gus are household names. Blue has a small Methodist Church and Gus has a sign with three letters– G-U-S (that's all I saw anyway). Here I was, literally in the middle of nowhere and Craig knew the next two towns coming up on a Farm to Market road!

As much as I was enjoying working with Craig, I did encourage him to slow down. He was based in Dallas until the late '90s but rarely turned down an opportunity to broadcast at any level. In addition to calling high school football and hosting two television programs, he also called indoor and outdoor soccer, and enthusiastically said yes when I asked him if he wanted to call Texas Women's Basketball. Legendary Baylor Bears play-by-play voice Frank Fallon once stepped into our booth and told Craig that he "couldn't do them all."

His work ethic, energy, and enthusiasm were unmatched, as was his ability to remember games, players, statistics, records, etc. His power of recall came into play years later when Craig came to Austin and was my co-host on Sports Day, an afternoon drive talk show on AM 1300 the Zone. During an in-studio visit with former Pro Bowl Quarterback John Hadl, Craig asked Hadl a detailed question about a Rams-Cowboys playoff game in 1973. About thirty seconds into Craig's question, Hadl interrupted, "Craig, I'm going to stop you right there, you already remember more about that game than I do."

That was pretty impressive since Hadl was playing for the Rams at the time, and Craig was a pre-teen in Greensboro, North Carolina. Perhaps my favorite Craig Way memory came during the NCAA basketball tournament in 1995. He was scheduled to work as a reporter for the Host/CBS Radio Network for the first and second-round games in Boise, Idaho. He was also my broadcast partner and analyst for the Longhorn Radio Network. The Longhorns were sent out west to Salt Lake City, where they would meet Oregon in a first-round game on a Thursday and would play again on Saturday if they won. The games in Boise were scheduled for Friday and Sunday.

He tried to secure flights between the two cities but was unable to do so. No problem. 339 miles separate Salt Lake City and Boise, so Craig just rented a car. After the Horns defeated Oregon 90-73 in the opening round, Craig and I went to dinner with some network executives. He then dropped me off at the team hotel and headed out to Boise.

I got a great night's sleep, woke up and took a shower. I then turned my television on as CBS was previewing each of the regions. As they were taking a look at the Boise region, which featured eventual national champion UCLA, I spotted Craig in the background sitting courtside in a coat and tie. I laughed out loud. How could this guy broadcast a game, eat dinner, drive five hours, maybe catch a couple of hours of sleep, and then make it to the arena in plenty of time for the games in that region? He then made the drive back to Salt Lake, helped me call the Maryland Terrapins' second-round win over Texas, and then headed back to Boise to cover UCLA's heart-stopping last-second win over Missouri.

That game featured a length of the court drive by Tyus Edney, who just barely beat the buzzer with a layup. When I asked Craig if he drove the speed limit while driving over 1,400 miles that weekend, he explained to me that he employed the art of binocular driving. Since it was so flat in parts of northern Utah, he would cruise at 95 miles per hour with one hand on the wheel, and the other hand holding binoculars, so he could see any other vehicles miles before they approached him. It was a typical Craig Way tactic.

I could take up many more pages describing the travel and broadcasting exploits of Craig Way, but I think I'll let him recount some of those tales in his own book one day. I can tell you that it was a joy to work with him and he made me a better broadcaster. I always considered myself a hard worker, but Craig took that term to an entirely new level.

# "The hardest working man in show business" • 133

*Craig Way was an excellent broadcast partner with an encyclopedic mind*

# 50

# Majerus

The Longhorn basketball team, at the time known as the Runnin' Horns, had gained a reputation for playing a tough nonconference schedule. Coach Tom Penders was trying to recruit players from New York and the east coast and he knew that network TV liked to televise intersectional games. UConn, North Carolina, LSU (during the Shaquille O'Neal era), and Arizona were among the top teams Texas played. In a game at Utah, I had the chance to interview the colorful Coach Rick Majerus, who was building a respected program in Salt Lake City.

I knew that Penders and Majerus had known each other a long time, so I asked Majerus about their relationship. I'll never forget his response, "I've known Tommy Penders forever, going all the way back to his early days, when he was coaching at that Catholic school in New York, Fordham. I know for a fact that the Catholic priest at the end of their bench was getting more action than Penders was." Needless to say, I had to do some editing of that interview. Thanks Coach!

51

## Tubbs

During the Penders era, Texas was consistently one of the top programs in the Southwest Conference. The Arkansas Razorbacks and the Texas Tech Red Raiders were also among the contenders. Texas Christian was also building up their program under former Oklahoma Head Coach Billy Tubbs. The Horned Frogs had defeated Texas in Fort Worth earlier in the season, and the second game at the Erwin Center was a critical game that would go a long way in determining the regular-season champion.

TCU featured star center Kurt Thomas, who led the nation in rebounding and scoring during the '94-95 season. In the game at Austin, the Runnin' Horns jumped out to a big lead early and cruised to a 111-99 win. Following the game, Coach Tubbs told his sports information director that he was not interested in doing any postgame interviews or any type of press conference. It took an effort, but the SID, Kent Johnson, finally talked Tubbs into walking down the hall to face the writers and TV cameras. Tubbs was not happy, "I was told I'm required to make an opening statement," he fumed, "We got our butt kicked, and now I'm going to take three questions." From the back of the room, a reporter yelled, "How come only three questions?" Tubbs quickly responded, "Now we're down to two questions."

# 52

## Zonk

Early in my tenure at KLBJ, when I was covering Longhorn baseball, I had the opportunity to develop a friendship with former major leaguer Keith Moreland. He was given the nickname "Zonk" by longtime teammate Larry Bowa, who was a very good shortstop for the Phillies and Cubs during his career. Bowa thought that Moreland physically resembled Miami Dolphins fullback Larry Csonka. The stocky Moreland did have a football background and had played "Monster Back" on the UT football team under coach Darrell Royal. Monster Back was a hybrid strong safety/linebacker.

Keith decided to give up his gridiron career after the arrival of running back Earl Campbell at UT. Shortly into Campbell's first scrimmage, the future Heisman trophy winner ran off tackle and ran right over Moreland, cracking his helmet. It wasn't long after that collision that Moreland told Coach Royal he was going to concentrate on baseball. Somebody else would have to tackle the "Tyler Rose" during practice every day. "Zonk" made the right decision. In 1975 the hard-hitting utility player helped lead the Longhorns to the national college baseball championship.

Following an 11-year major league career, Moreland returned to Austin and became a volunteer assistant coach for Cliff Gustafson. I enjoyed our pregame visits and told him if he ever wanted to give broadcasting a try, I'd love to have him join me in the booth. Several years later, he took me up on my offer. I'm proud to say that Zonk is still broadcasting baseball and football, 27 years later.

One of my favorite Zonk stories was during a rainout in Ames, Iowa. The Longhorns and Iowa State Cyclones were scheduled to play a three-game series. When the Friday afternoon game was rained out, we now had an off day and night in Ames, Iowa. Woohoo! Now what? The previous day, in a joking manner, I asked my talk show partner Craig Way what there was to do in Ames in the event of a rainout. He laughed and suggested the Bob Feller Museum in Van Meter, Iowa.

Feller was a major league pitcher who had one of the highest velocity fastballs of all time, earning the nickname "Rapid Robert." As we were leaving the ballpark on the Iowa State campus early that Friday afternoon, I mentioned the Feller Museum to Zonk. Since we didn't have a lot of options in Ames, Zonk pulled out an Iowa map, and before I knew it, we headed west on state highway 30, and then south on state highway 17 and on our way to the tiny town of Van Meter (pop. 1,131), about an hour away.

The Feller museum had lots of photos and memorabilia from his playing career. There were also artifacts from his four years of service in the U.S. Navy during WWII. After the museum visit and lunch in Van Meter, we were on our way back to Ames until Zonk and I heard an announcement on the radio that got our attention. "Tonight it's opening night at Prairie Downs in Des Moines. Come check out live thoroughbred racing. 6 pm post time! Don't miss it!" Zonk was driving and turned to me with wide-eyed amazement. He then gave me a high five, took the next immediate right-hand turn (on some farm-to-market road) and we meandered through the back roads of central Iowa on our way to Prairie Downs.

We arrived at 5:40 pm, with plenty of time to get our bets in for the daily double. A few years later, in 2000, Texas qualified for the College World Series in Omaha, Nebraska. The academic year was already over, so my 16-year-old son Eric traveled with Zonk and me to Omaha. We landed around 2:30 in the afternoon, and I was scheduled to do my talk show from the legendary Rosenblatt Stadium, starting at 4 pm. Zonk loved to play the ponies and dogs and knew of a dog track just across the Missouri River in Council Bluffs, Iowa. He dropped me off at the ballpark and treated Eric to an afternoon of Greyhound Racing at Horseshoe Council Bluffs.

Back at Rosenblatt, I tracked down Harold Reynolds to be a guest on the show. Reynolds, a former major league infielder with the Seattle Mariners, was a solid broadcaster and would be covering the series for ESPN, which aired every game live. The eight-team tournament was starting the next day, but Harold and his crewmates had been there for a few days, watching batting practice and team drills. During the interview, I asked Harold to "handicap the field." He responded, "Oh, the field is in great shape, I know the groundskeeper from my playing days, and the field is good." Uh, that's not exactly what I meant.

Down in the parking lot, the state of Louisiana was taking over. The Ragin' Cajuns of Louisiana-Lafayette and the LSU Tigers both qualified that year, and their fans had driven up from the Bayou, and they were ready to tailgate. It was a classic case of "laissez les bon temps rouler" (let the good times roll) with big pots of gumbo and etouffee, and endless pitchers of frozen daiquiris, complete with a background soundtrack of Zydeco music. The Cajuns created a Mardi Gras-like atmosphere.

Across the river in Council Bluffs, it was a very windy day and apparently the conditions were making it difficult to pick winning dogs. Long shots were coming in all day. It was not a fruitful few hours for Zonk and Eric, who made it back to Omaha to pick me up after my talk show. While at the stadium, I had picked up credentials, tournament media guides, rosters and schedules.

On our way to the hotel, I opened the guide to the section containing College World Series records. At the time Zonk had the most hits in CWS history. I then asked the trivia question out loud, "Who holds the College World Series record for total hits?" Zonk smiled proudly and said, "Well that would be... ME!" If my broadcast partner was despondent after losing a few bucks at the Horseshoe Dog Track, he quickly got over it. I still work an occasional college baseball game here and there, and I honestly do miss broadcasting baseball, and especially miss the rapport that I enjoyed when I called games with Keith Moreland, who remains a good friend.

*Former major league baseball player Keith Moreland has a ton of funny stories*

## 53

## The Lost weekend

In September of 1997, I was optimistic about the football season. Texas was coming off a Big XII Championship season, was ranked #11 in the country, and boasted one of the best running backs in the nation in junior Ricky Williams. I was also happy that I was getting a chance to call major league baseball on Sundays. Eric Nadel, the longtime radio voice of the Texas Rangers, had enlisted me to help when his broadcast partner at the time, Brad Sham, had a conflict with CBS Radio NFL coverage. When the Longhorns hosted UCLA on September 13th, I was geared up for a fun weekend, since I'd be flying to Arlington the next day for a Sunday afternoon game between the Rangers and Minnesota Twins.

The Longhorn game was an absolute disaster. Turnovers, missed tackles, and dropped passes plagued the Longhorns. The Bruins led 38-0 at the half, on their way to a 66-3 win. It remains the worst loss in the history of the Texas football program. After a postgame call-in show that was full of vitriol and demands that Coach John Mackovic be fired, I was ready for a couple of glasses of wine.

At least I had the Ranger broadcast the next day to get my mind off the debacle that I had just described on the 74 station Texas Longhorn Radio Network. I caught an early Sunday morning flight from Austin to DFW, got to the Ballpark in Arlington early so I could visit with some players and get the lineups for both teams.

Former pitcher Bert Blyleven was the Twins television analyst and I introduced myself as we were writing down the lineups in the media room. I remember Blyleven as an excellent curveball pitcher with the Minnesota Twins and Pittsburgh Pirates. In fact, only four pitchers in major league history have recorded more strikeouts than Blyleven. After a brief introduction, he noticed my golf shirt.

Blyleven: "Is that a Longhorn logo on your shirt?'
BS: "Yes it is Bert, I'm the radio voice of the Texas Longhorns."
Blyleven: "You mean, you're the voice of the team that got their ass kicked 66-3 yesterday?"
BS: "Well, I guess I am."
Blyleven: "You've got some balls wearing that today."

He said it with a big smile, and I chuckled as well, but honestly didn't see as much humor in his statement as he did. A few minutes later I was in the radio booth and doing final game prep, and I looked to my left. Adjacent to our booth, separated only by a pane of glass, was Bert Blyleven and the Twins TV crew. Blyleven smiled and waved, and then, with a pair of scissors, started cutting up his copy of the Sunday edition of the Dallas Morning News. He carefully cut out every picture and headline related to the Texas loss to UCLA. With scotch tape he started hanging the newspaper strips, making sure the headlines and pictures were staring at me the entire game.

It was hard to get mad at him because he was doing it all with a smile on his face. Then the game started and the Rangers looked like the Longhorns had the day before. They couldn't do anything right. The Twins hit the ball all over the field. The Rangers looked lethargic and disinterested in an ugly 11-1 loss. As Nadel and I were wrapping up our broadcast after the game, Blyleven wrote a handmade sign on the back of a lineup card and hung it up. He then tapped on the window to get my attention, smiled broadly and pointed to his sign, which read in big bold letters, "Nice Weekend Bill. 77 to 4!"

## Daryl Hamilton

One September Sunday afternoon in 1996, about two hours prior to a Texas Rangers broadcast, I conducted a pregame interview with outfielder Daryl Hamilton, a veteran player who had played collegiately at Nicholls State in Thibodaux, Louisiana. Ten years earlier, I had seen Hamilton play a game at Holleman Field in Huntsville, Texas against Sam Houston State.

For my final question of the interview, I told Hamilton that a crowd of 30,000 was expected at the Ballpark at Arlington that afternoon, and then asked him how many folks in the crowd that day may have seen him play for Nicholls State. He quickly answered "Zero."

I was proud to correct him and tell him "Well, actually, the answer is one - me!" We shared a laugh and I then concluded the interview. He went on to play five more seasons in the majors and eventually became a broadcaster. Sadly, Daryl Hamilton was the victim of a murder-suicide in 2015.

I never thought I'd ever have the opportunity to sing with a gospel choir, but when I wrote "Second Chance" I knew I would need some soulful support on vocals. When I heard the choir from the Wesley United Methodist Church sing at a praise service, I was very impressed, and just bold enough to approach the choir director LaMonica Lewis about helping me out.

Without hesitation and with no negotiation whatsoever, LaMonica quickly agreed and a few days later brought several choir members to Nic Whitworth's studio. They sang backup on two original tunes, "Second Chance" and "Down in the Valley." They were fun to work with, and possessed amazing musical acumen, understanding exactly where Nic and I were going with the lyric, melody, and rhythm.

The song itself is about the beauty of second chances and fresh starts, something all of us may need at some point. I know I certainly did.

---

**"Second Chance"**

*Your world was falling all around you*

*You were drowning in your mistakes*

*Living life in the fast lane   You refused to hit the brakes*

*You had to slow down and looked up to the sky*

*There was the Lord drying tears from your eyes*

*Chorus*

*Will you laugh will you sing will you dance?*

*What are you doin' with your second chance?*

*Will you make a difference? Will you take a stance?*

*What are you doin' with your second chance?*

*Trapped in a corner*

*You didn't know your fate*

*Wailing cries of forgiveness   Given a clean slate*

*It's time that you share all that he's done*

*Just look at you   how far you've come*

*Repeat chorus 2X*

*We're laughing   we're singing   we're dancing*

*What are you doin'?*

---

The talented musicians who supported me on "Second Chance"

## Mackovic

At the start of the 1992 Longhorn football season, I took over as the play-by-play voice after serving as the analyst for two seasons. I got to work alongside Brad Sham in 1990 and Jerry Trupiano in 1991, and learned lots from both of them. My first game in the play-by-play chair coincided with the start of John Mackovic's tenure as head coach. He came to UT from the University of Illinois and had previously coached the Kansas City Chiefs.

Although he had a reputation of being somewhat snobbish, I got along with Mackovic just fine. He invited me to play in various golf outings and asked me to serve as emcee for a few football related functions. I hosted his weekly statewide radio show during his entire six-year tenure. One day at a preseason training camp practice he pulled up to me in a golf cart, and asked me to ride with him. We watched the different position groups go through their drills.

I was wondering why he was being so nice. Actually, he remembered I had undergone a vasectomy procedure the day before and he figured I was sore. He was right. I truly appreciated that gesture. He had his moments of sarcasm, too. One day during a golf scramble at Barton Creek Country Club, I hit one of the best three woods I ever hit, reaching a long par five in 2. Our team would be putting for eagle!

Mackovic complimented my shot, and proclaimed loudly that I was probably the second best left-handed golfer he had played with. When I asked who was best, he retorted, "Every other lefty golfer I've played with is tied for first."

There were occasions when I saw the "uppity" side as well. One night before the radio show he told me had just watched some game film with the radio audio as a soundtrack. He told me I should describe a short pass between the hash marks as "across the middle" instead of "over the middle". I figured if that's the worst thing I did during the game broadcast, I must be ok.

One evening he surprised me and invited me to dinner after the statewide show. We dined at the Old San Francisco Steakhouse. When I ordered a Pinot Grigio with a New York Strip, the coach was not pleased. He reminded me that white wine pairs with chicken or fish and red wine would be better suited for the steak. It was then that the Southwest Philly in me almost came out. Really? You're going to second guess my wine pairing? I instead just brushed it off, but assured the waitress that I STILL wanted the white wine with the red meat, even if it somehow offended my dining partner, who was particular about his wine. I was very tempted to change my order to a nice glass of Boone's Farm, just to see Mackovic's reaction.

A few years later, the Longhorns made a coaching change and Mack Brown replaced Mackovic, who remained in Austin for a few years while working for ESPN as a studio analyst on Saturdays. Early in the 1998 season, the Horns lost at Kansas State. I stayed in Kansas City and flew commercially the next day back to Austin. At the time I was a frequent flyer on American Airlines and was often eligible for upgrades to first class. I called the airline on Saturday and was able to get the last available first-class seat between Dallas and Austin (the second leg of my return flight).

While the flight from DFW to Austin was boarding, I settled into the first-class cabin and had already begun sipping a vodka and orange juice when I heard a familiar voice. It was the voice of John Mackovic, who was on his way back to Austin after a full day Saturday at ESPN in Bristol, Connecticut. I assumed he was also in first class, and I thought for a moment I would switch with another passenger so I could visit with the coach during the flight. When I asked him where he was sitting, he responded that someone called the day before and got the last seat available in first class (that would've been me) so he was headed to the back of the plane.

Perhaps because I had already consumed a vodka and orange juice, I just couldn't resist bidding him adieu from the first-class cabin, as I said loudly, "Well, have a good time back in coach, Coach!" A few years later, when Mackovic was hired as the head coach at the University of Arizona, Craig invited him to join us on our talk show. After the usual pleasantries to start the interview, the coach told Craig he couldn't remember the last time he saw me. "Oh, I remember John," I said, "I was in 2A and you were on your way back to 29 C."

*John Mackovic didn't show his sense of humor often, but he could be quite charming at times.*

---

56

---

## Two places at once

---

In May of 1993, I got a call from Top Rank, the boxing promoters handling the WBO Heavyweight Championship bout between Tommy Morrison and 44-year-old former champ George Foreman. We arranged a phone interview with Top Rank president Bob Arum. The bout was still a few weeks away but Arum was trying to drum up early interest in the match. The interview went well. I guess I impressed Arum in some way because the next day I got another call from the Top Rank folks, and I was invited to Las Vegas for the fight.

Top Rank was going to issue me a credential for the bout, pay for my airfare and provide a room at the Hilton (where the fight was taking place). I accepted the invitation right away, and airline tickets were mailed to me. The only caveat was that the Texas Longhorn baseball team was playing very well in the postseason. If the Horns were to somehow win their regional tournament and qualify for the College World Series in Omaha, I would have a conflict. I couldn't be in Omaha and Las Vegas at the same time.

Well, as fate would have it, Coach Cliff Gustafson's Longhorns defeated the USC Trojans in the finals of the NCAA Central

Regional and the Horns (and their radio play-by-play guy) were headed to Omaha. I was now in possession of an airline ticket from Austin to Vegas for a heavyweight title fight, but I wouldn't be able to attend. My buddy Bobby Ray, an evening disc jockey for KLBJ FM, had a solution. He offered to go to the bout as Bill Schoening. Remember, this was eight years before 9/11. Airline and airport security was rather relaxed. As far as I knew, Bob Arum and the Top Rank folks had no idea what I looked like.

I didn't want the airline ticket to go to waste so I gave it to Bobby. He flew to Vegas, spent three nights at the Hilton, rubbed elbows with Burt Sugar and Angelo Dundee, and witnessed Morrison defeat Foreman by unanimous decision, all while wearing a credential that featured his picture but my name. To this day, Bobby keeps that credential displayed at his house. He says it was good to be Bill Schoening for a weekend. For me, it was the only time I got to cover a title fight. Well, sort of.

# Spike

One of my favorite guys ever is the late Texas Tech Head Football Coach Spike Dykes. Born in the small West Texas town of Ballinger, Spike earned a football scholarship at Stephen F. Austin State and then worked his way up the ranks as a Texas high school coach at exotic locations like Coahoma, Eastland, and Alice. After a number of college assistant coaching jobs, he was named head coach at Texas Tech in 1987.

For some reason, Spike and I hit it off, partly because he thought it was cool that the voice of the Longhorns was once the voice of the Lamesa Golden Tornadoes. He had driven through Lamesa countless times on Highway 87 south of Tahoka and north of Big Spring. Spike was extremely bright but made you think he was a country bumpkin.

In 1989, I covered a Texas Tech at Texas game in which the Red Raiders pulled off a 24-17 upset in front of a packed house at Darrell K Royal Texas Memorial Stadium. With his players hoisting him up on their shoulders, a reporter asked Dykes if it was the biggest win in his coaching career. Without hesitation, he said, "Oh no, when I was at Coahoma, we beat Colorado City in Bi-District."

Spike's relationship with Texas Coach John Mackovic was very unique. They were polar opposites in many ways, but there was a mutual respect when it came to football. The best illustration of their different personas came in the summer of 1994 when Coach Mackovic teamed with a local travel agency in Austin to organize a weeklong trip to the French Wine Country. Mackovic recorded the radio commercial himself, inviting Longhorn fans to join him and his wife Arlene for, "Golf during the day, followed by chardonnay and sauvignon blanc in the evenings."

When I scheduled Coach Dykes to join me by phone for a fifteen-minute interview, I thought it might be cool to play the commercial on air so Spike could hear it just prior to our segment. After airing the commercial, I welcomed Spike back to the show and asked him if he was considering the European excursion with Coach Mackovic. "I'd love to join John and Arlene over there in France for their wine deal, but I'm afraid I got me a conflict. That same week we've got us a "Beef and Beer" at the Floydada Country Club. Now, I know what you're thinking- - they only have nine holes at the Floydada Country Club. Well, that's true, but don't worry - we're gonna go around twice." Coach Dykes retired after the 1999 season and died in 2017 at the age of 79. If I had to list my favorite opposing coaches through the years, he'd be right at the top.

## Fourth and inches

Prior to the start of the '96-'97 academic year Texas, Texas Tech, Baylor and Texas A&M left the Southwest Conference to join the Big 8 schools and formed the Big XII. We knew the Horns would be stepping up in class. I couldn't wait to call a baseball game at Oklahoma State, a basketball game at Kansas, and a football game at Nebraska. I would get the chance in short order, but not before calling the first Big XII Championship game between South Division champ Texas and North Division champ - the powerful and third-ranked Nebraska Cornhuskers.

The game was played on a neutral field, at the TWA Dome in St. Louis, but 90% of the crowd was pulling for Nebraska and wearing red. The Cornhuskers were 21 point favorites, but the Longhorns outplayed the Huskers most of the game and were clinging to a 30-27 lead with 2:30 remaining in the fourth quarter. Texas faced a fourth and inches at its own 29-yard line. Instead of punting, Head Coach John Mackovic decided to go for it. In one of the most famous plays in the storied program's history, Quarterback James Brown faked a handoff, rolled to his left out of a power I formation, and then lofted the ball downfield to wide-open tight end Derek Lewis for a 61 yard gain.

On-air I bellowed, "Do you believe that? John Mackovic, rolling the dice and picking up 61 yards!" Analyst Craig Way added, "That may have been the gutsiest call in John Mackovic's coaching career." On the very next play, running back Priest Holmes followed the block of All America guard Dan Neil and scampered 10 yards into the end zone, securing a 37-27 upset win. I've called hundreds of football games in my career, but the inaugural Big XII championship game is my favorite. Years later, a fellow told me that he graduated from UT that same day. Apparently, many folks at the graduation ceremonies were listening to the radio broadcast with earbuds in. At the moment his name was announced, the Horns came up with that big play on fourth and inches. At first he thought the loud eruption in the crowd was for his academic achievement, but quickly realized it was more about the football game. From my perspective, it was good to know I had a captive audience that day!

# The Zone

As early as 1993 I thought Austin was big enough to support an all-sports station. I was unable to convince management at KLBJ to put local and national sports on the FM signal (93.3) they owned. In 1995, when the Longhorn Broadcast rights went across town to KVET, the new flagship station's management was much more aggressive in its approach to sports coverage and sports marketing. The games were put on FM and AM, and staff was increased.

By 1998, it was clear that an all-sports station might work. KVET AM would now be full-time sports, with an emphasis on local coverage. To promote the new station, nine full and part-time staffers were willing to pose nude for a billboard and print ad campaign, with the strategic parts hidden by a banner. The front-facing billboard read "Total Sports Coverage," and the picture from behind was "Nothing Butt Sports." Contrary to a rumor that has floated around for years, each of us wore our boxers or briefs during the shoot. We also wore black socks for special effect.

A billboard on I-35 near Darrell K Royal Texas Memorial Stadium caught the attention of *Texas Monthly Magazine*. The picture of nine naked male sportscasters won the "Bum Steer Award" from Texas Monthly for worst ad campaign. We were very proud of that. The willingness to bare it all for the station got us some statewide publicity. Mission accomplished!

In the early days of the station, it's safe to say we needed to reel it in just a tad. One December morning I was in Tulsa for a Texas vs. Oral Roberts University basketball game to be played that evening. David Anderson and Hugh Lewis were co-hosting the late morning show back at the station. During the Longhorn shootaround at the ORU Arena, I called in to the show to preview the game. My timing apparently wasn't very good. The last thing on the minds of my coworkers that morning was college basketball.

Producer Mike Pirtle had arranged an in-studio appearance by adult film star Kylie Ireland, who was in town and performing at a local men's club. Apparently, David was getting a lap dance while I was attempting to break down the keys to the game that night. For some reason, he seemed distracted. After a minute or two I wrapped up my segment quickly, promoted the game broadcast, and allowed the fellows to return to their shenanigans.

The station was quickly becoming partly sports talk, and partly "guy" talk. Although Craig and I usually stuck to sports on our afternoon show, we were both big music fans and on Fridays, we would preview some bands and artists to catch in Austin, while also picking out the best band names from the Austin Chronicle. A few of our favorites were Big Ass Truck, I Love you but I've Chosen Darkness, Euripides Pants, and They'll Know Us By The Trail of Dead. Working at an all-sports station like the Zone was a blast because there were so few rules, and we had a knack for breaking those rules anyway.

*Nine naked sports guys*

## Austin Ice Bats

Only once during my career did I get to cover a professional hockey team. Well, I sort of covered them, and they were sort of professional. The Austin Ice Bats were among a handful of teams that comprised the fledgling Western Professional Hockey League, with other franchises starting up in well-known hockey hotbeds such as Amarillo, Odessa, and Albuquerque. Even though the WPHL would be classified as low minors, I had a feeling hockey might work in Austin. The town was growing and not everyone in the city was a "dyed in the wool" Texas Longhorn.

Hockey has always been a sport much better seen live than on television. There were no pro sports in Austin. The Round Rock Express, to be based in Williamson County just north of Austin, was still a few years away from taking the field. When former NHL player Blaine Stoughton decided to put a hockey team in Austin, he knew he had to educate the public, so I invited him to join me on our afternoon talk show. Having grown up in Philly during the height of the Flyers' Stanley Cup championship days, I knew the sport pretty well.

Blaine and I struck up a friendship, and he became a regular on the show- answering fans' questions about the team, the league, and most importantly, the rules. If you grew up in East Austin, there's really no reason you should know what icing is. We conducted Hockey 101, but Blaine was entertaining, and always had dozens of tickets to give away to station staff and listeners. He figured if he could get folks in the seats they would come back and pay for the privilege the next time. He was right. They'd also buy beers (and plenty of them), jerseys, and hot dogs.

About a week before the first game in Ice Bats history, Blaine finalized a deal with KVUE-TV in Austin to televise this "momentous" event. After his appearance on the radio show that night, Blaine asked me if I'd be interested in calling the play-by-play on KVUE. I had never broadcast a hockey game before, but I was Blaine's choice. Honestly, I would've done that gig for free. I was enjoying my new relationship with all these friendly Canadians who were trying to sell a sport to an audience I knew very well. I was thrilled that he chose me to call the opening game and I was looking forward to the challenge.

Before I could throw a dollar figure at him, he proposed a $500 talent fee. Knowing that box seats were going for about $25 a pop, I suggested he pay me $400 and give me four seats on the glass. It was a very quick negotiation. My family got to sit in the front row, while I called the game on KVUE TV, with a raucous crowd of over 6,000 at the Travis County Expo Center, which would soon be known as The Bat Cave. I ended up broadcasting only a few more Ice bats games.

There were no more TV broadcasts, but I did get to pinch-hit for Mark Martello on the radio a few times. I got to know the players very well because we had a regular weekly Ice Bats segment on the radio show. The players were mostly young guys from western Canada, and very few, if any, had NHL potential.

On air, they were loose and eager to tell stories, which is always welcome in sports radio.

Rookie defenseman Ryan Anderson came to the station one afternoon and talked about growing up in Bowsman, Manitoba. When I asked where Bowsman was located geographically, he was ready. Purposely exaggerating a thick Canadian accent, Anderson replied, "Bowsman? Where a boats is Bowsman, eh? Well if you know a boats where Winnipeg is, it's a boat an eight-hour drive north. It's a small farming town." I fell right into his trap. "They have farms eight hours north of Winnipeg? What can they possibly grow?" The one-word answer came as if on cue, "Icicles."

On occasion, I'd take the family or some friends to a game as a fan. The Bat Cave had a "Bat Loft" for postgame drinks with the players. It was common to see players from the opposing team drinking and hanging with Ice Bat players, even if they had been brawling with each other an hour earlier. They were like one big fraternity. Winger Jeff Gabriel came to the studio one afternoon for a segment on the show and saw my Ibanez guitar in the corner. I was about to upgrade to a beautiful cherrywood Takemine in just a few days.

Jeff complained during the show about how the Ice Bats' long bus rides were tedious and boring. I asked him on-air if he might want to borrow the Ibanez for the rest of the season. He was very appreciative and took the guitar, along with its soft canvass case. For the next three months, my poor little acoustic guitar was strummed, plucked, banged around, dropped, thrown, and apparently one drunken night in Amarillo, it was used as a goalie stick.

When Jeff returned the guitar (without its case) and missing two strings, complete with dents and nicks everywhere, he said, "The boys fell in love with your guitar." Honestly, the Takemine was such an upgrade that I had no plans for the Ibanez anyway. I will say this, however. I have never lent a guitar to a hockey team again. For some reason, I had a soft spot in my heart for these players. I felt bad that these guys were so far away from home during Thanksgiving, so I asked Gerry if we could host four of the players for a nice dinner on Thanksgiving afternoon.

When she said yes, I extended invitations to four players, and each player asked if I would have beer at my house. I assured all four guys I would have plenty of beer. I personally don't drink the stuff, but I got a case of Molson and a case of Labatt's. You know, Canadian beers for these Canucks. When I answered the door upon their arrival, each player had a six-pack of beer. Even though I had assured each of them I would be well-stocked, they wanted to take NO chances. Beer is apparently very important to young hockey players from Alberta and Saskatchewan.

When I reminded defenseman Kyle "Havs" Haviland that I would have beer he shrugged and said, "You can never be too careful, eh?" The most interesting moment of conversation during dinner revolved around the flattened nose of Haviland, who was the team's enforcer and league leader in penalty minutes. He was one of the older guys on the team and was a hockey minor league journeyman.

When I asked him if he was concerned about the condition of his nose, he laughed it off and said, "Hell, my nose has now been broken eight times. Why should I worry about it? I know there's going to be a ninth." The Ice Bats and the WPHL are now defunct, but for a brief time, they provided Austin with some entertaining minor league hockey and some welcome Canadian flavor.

## Run Run Ricky

During my career, I have been able to describe every play in the amazing Hall of Fame careers of two players. One was Spurs guard Manu Ginobili, who will one day be in the Naismith Memorial Basketball Hall of Fame. The other is College Football Hall of Famer Ricky Williams. The colorful, dreadlocked Williams broke Tony Dorsett's longstanding (22 years) NCAA Division I career rushing record when he went on a 60-yard scamper for a touchdown against arch-rival Texas A&M in 1998.

When Ricky's four-year career at Texas was over, he was the all-time leading scorer in NCAA history with 452 points. He had scored 73 rushing touchdowns, also a record. Williams rushed for 200 yards or more on 12 different occasions. Ricky may have been a little different or quirky, but I loved the guy. When John Mackovic got fired after Ricky's junior year, most of us figured Ricky would just opt for the NFL, but new Head Coach Mack Brown was somehow able to talk Ricky into staying, and he ended up rushing for 2,327 yards and 29 touchdowns his senior year.

While Ricky was zeroing in on Tony Dorsett's rushing record, my friend Jimmy LaFave, a popular Austin singer/songwriter, called me one day and played me a song over the phone. He had rewritten The Chuck Berry Classic "Run Run Rudolph" with the lyrics befitting the Longhorn running back's pursuit of the rushing record and the Heisman Trophy. I invited Jimmy to debut "Run Run Ricky" on our radio show. KVUE TV then produced a video that was shown on the giant message board at the stadium.

There were billboards on I-35 cheering Ricky on. Our station started giving away Run Run Ricky T-shirts. He graced the cover of *Sports Illustrated*. One year after the 66-3 loss to UCLA and its ugly aftermath, here was the City of Austin coming together to celebrate a truly special athlete. What a difference a year makes! In December, Ricky Williams was awarded the Heisman Trophy, the second player in Longhorn history to earn the honor, joining the legendary Earl Campbell. Ricky broke many of Earl's long standing records at Texas, and it was a joy to cover the entirety of his amazing college career.

*Ricky Williams was the best football player I ever covered*

# Earl

Since we're on the subject of the two most famous running backs in UT history, here are a few words about the Tyler Rose, Earl Christian Campbell. The first time I saw Earl in person was during my Sam Houston State days. KSAM morning man Kooter Roberson had received a tip about a private show Willie Nelson was putting on at a club called the Longhorn Saloon in Cut 'N Shoot, about 30 miles away. Yes, the name of the town is Cut 'N Shoot. We were told it was BYOB so we stopped at a liquor store to get beer for Kooter and wine for me.

The small venue was crowded but we had a table in the back, which was still less than 100 feet from the stage. Just before the music started, I noticed Earl in the front row. I later learned that he had come over to the gig on the Willie tour bus from Austin. It was a hip crowd with lots of media and radio types, so nobody bothered Earl as he jammed to Willie and the Family while drinking cans of beer. Earl started forming a pyramid with his empties, and before the end of the night, it was a pretty impressive display of beer drinking and aluminum construction. Pharoah would've been proud of this pyramid!

When I got to Austin a few years later, Earl was always around the university, at various functions, and at ballgames. He had been on my show several times and was always friendly and usually funny. In the late 90's Craig and I had a weekly remote location for our 4-7 pm show at a restaurant called UR Cook's. Earl agreed to come on so we promoted his appearance and the restaurant was packed when we started the show. Earl enjoyed a couple of beers as we chatted about Bum Phillips, Luv Ya Blue and Willie Nelson.

Without warning, he asked me if the station had a version of "You Never Even Called Me By Name," a cult country hit by David Allan Coe. Back at the station, producer Chad Hastings tracked it down. When we returned from a commercial break, Chad cued up the tune, Earl led the entire restaurant to a rousing rendition. It was impromptu, uneven, and a bit off-key but the live audience loved it. I'm sure it wasn't quite as appealing to our listening audience, but sometimes bad radio is good radio. It was honestly never on my bucket list to sing a country song on the radio at a restaurant with Earl Campbell, but if it was, I could now scratch that baby off the list.

# 63

# LaFave

Shortly after arriving in Austin, I wanted to check out the local music scene. I had heard so much about the "Live Music Capital of the World," I wanted to see and hear it for myself. My buddy Bobby Ray had been the evening deejay at rock station KLBJ-FM, and then moved to KGSR, a station that played a mixture of folk, rock, jazz, and world music, with special attention paid to Texas singer/songwriters. I learned a lot about Texas music from KGSR. One of the artists featured regularly was Jimmy LaFave, a native Oklahoman who had just moved to Austin. His music was somewhat reminiscent of his early music heroes, Woody Guthrie and Bob Dylan.

Jimmy's voice was perfect for the sensitive love ballads he wrote. I bought a CD called "Austin Skyline," and caught a show at the Cactus Café, an intimate "listening room" on the UT campus. When I introduced myself after the gig, Jimmy told me he was a sports fan and had listened to my show and to some of the Longhorn football games. We struck up a friendship. Several times, when Oklahoma State came to Austin for football or basketball, I would snare him a couple of tickets. In return, Jimmy would put me on the guest list for his shows.

By the late '90s, when I started to play guitar and write songs of my own, he was nice enough to listen to me over the phone as I banged out a few basic chords and sang the early stages of my songs to him. He would almost always say, "I like where you're TRYING to go with that." Even though my evening talk show centered on sports, I would invite Jimmy to come on occasionally and play a tune or promote an upcoming show.

In 2001, I was working on my first CD with producer Gabe Rhodes, and I somehow talked Jimmy into singing harmony vocals on a song I wrote called "Desolation Boardwalk." From that point on, whenever I attended one of his shows, he would acknowledge my presence. It became a regular theme as he would announce to the crowd something along these lines, "In the audience tonight is sportscaster Bill Schoening. Bill also writes songs. His CD 'Life in the Minors' is a million -seller- he's got a million in his cellar. In 2001, he talked me into singing backup on that record. I've done many things in music through the years, but I must say, in all honesty, singing on that Bill Schoening CD is the low point of my career."

Of course, the audience laughed every time at my expense, but I did too. Jimmy's delivery was always on point. I did figure out a way I could get some revenge. Whenever anyone told me they were going to see a LaFave show, I'd tell them to make sure they said hello, and then ask him, "Hey, aren't you Bill Schoening's backup singer?" In 2014, I went to see a LaFave Show at Threadgill's in Austin. I didn't tell Jimmy I was coming. I paid for my ticket, and then went to the back of the venue so he wouldn't see me, and therefore, wouldn't go through his routine of trying to embarrass me.

His drummer Bobby Kallus spotted me at one point, and then Jimmy then announced to the sellout crowd that there was a "celebrity" in the audience. I knew what was coming next. He started his familiar spiel, but this time (since the Spurs had just won the NBA title a few months earlier) he added that I would allow the ladies in attendance to kiss my NBA championship ring. At the end of his set, the crowd wanted more music and cheered for another song.

For an encore, the band played a cover version of Creedence Clearwater Revival's, "Have You Ever Seen the Rain?" As the band started to play, Jimmy urged me to get up on stage and sing with him. It's a good thing I knew the lyrics to that tune. Sadly, three years later, Jimmy died of cancer at the age of 61. For the next several months, I could not listen to a Jimmy LaFave song without the tears flowing.

Onstage with Jimmy LaFave

---

On the road one night in downtown Philly (The Spurs were playing the 76ers the following night) I was waiting for my singer/songwriter buddy Kenn Kweder at Mace's Crossing, a bar on Cherry Street near the team hotel. I was a few minutes early, so I ordered a glass of wine and observed the lively bar scene while waiting on Kenn. It was then that I noticed an elderly gentleman by himself chomping on an unlit cigar and making no eye contact with anyone. He looked like he was thinking about something or someone in the distant past.

The room was crowded and loud, but he was staring off into space and disconnected. When Kenn arrived at the bar we went upstairs, where there was a dining room. I soon forgot about the old man at the end of the bar. When I got back to my hotel room a few hours later, I had a melody stuck in my head so I sat down at the desk and wrote lyrics to fit the tune. My mind went back a few hours to the melancholy guy at Mace's Crossing. In the song I actually approach the gentleman, but in real life that didn't happen. This is among the saddest of my songs.

---

**"Unlit Cigar"**

*There's an old man at the end of the bar*

*He stares straight ahead with an unlit cigar*

*His eyes lack expression but they hint of pain*

*There are people around but he's lonely again*

*Chorus*

*What was on his mind?*

*A lover who left him somewhere down the line*

*Is there a clock he can rewind?*

*He needs to see her face just one more time*

*Bartender pours him a beer*

*No words are exchanged    Now I see a tear*

*The patrons   they just leave him alone*

*There with his thoughts from a time long gone*

*Repeat Chorus*

*I walked over and reached out my hand*

*He shook it and said "Do you understand?"*

*This pain deep inside   it won't go away*

*Because here in my heart is where she stays*

*Repeat Chorus*

## "Me and Daddy"

For six years I worked for KLBJ, which was owned by Lady Bird Johnson, widow of the late President. I got to meet Mrs. Johnson on several occasions and she would always be accompanied by two secret servicemen. She was very gracious and spoke with a soft southern accent. Her daughter Lucy was around quite a bit and maintained an office on the second floor. In 1994, KLBJ AM had a big night at the annual AP Awards dinner. Several folks in our news department were recognized for their work and I won a plaque for my play-by-play of Texas Longhorn football.

Lucy invited all of the winners to her beautiful home which was located adjacent to the 8th fairway at the Austin Country Club. At one point in the evening, Lucy wanted to show me her favorite hallway, which was lined with photos of her father, the 36th President of the United States. Lucy always referred to LBJ as 'daddy,' and Lady Bird was 'mother.' As we walked down the hall Lucy would stop every few feet, and point out the folks in these photos. Maybe because I was a sports guy she must've thought I didn't know anything about world or American history.

"Now Bill," she boasted, "this is a picture of me and daddy, and that man in the funny hat is Pope Paul VI. He was the head of the whole Catholic Church. This one is me and daddy and his vice president Hubert Humphrey, and this is a favorite of mine, it's me and daddy and Charles de Gaulle, who was the president of France and was a general during World War II." I was very respectful, but I really wanted to let Lucy know that even though I was a sports guy, I knew who these people were!

I went to Catholic school for twelve years so I was somewhat familiar with the Pope, I clearly remember Humphrey running for president against Richard Nixon in 1968, and I was a bit of a World War II buff, so yes, I did know about Charles de Gaulle as well. Nonetheless, it was a nice gesture to host us for dinner and take me for a stroll down her "favorite hallway."

A year later, KLBJ lost the broadcasting rights to UT Sports. For over a week, I weighed my options. Should I go across town to KVET and keep announcing the Longhorn games, or should I stay at KLBJ and continue hosting my evening talk show? KLBJ management offered me a nice little package, but I was a play by play guy, and simply could not give up the Longhorns. Although I chose to go across town, I'll never forget Lucy calling me into her office and asking me to stay, because she said I was "like family." So I guess for a six year period, I belonged to a pretty well-known family.

## 65

## Turning Down Nadia

When I got settled in across town at KVET Radio, I had a partner on the new talk show. General Manager Ron Rogers thought it would be good to pair me with Jeff Ward, a former Longhorn kicker who was already hosting his own show. In all honesty, Jeff and I both would've preferred having our own programs, but Rogers thought the differences in our ages, personalities and philosophies would make for good radio. It did.

We got along just fine but rarely agreed on any given topic. The *Austin Chronicle* named our show the best talk show in Austin that year. One of our guests was the legendary gymnast Nadia Comaneci. Nadia was on a tour promoting the Danskin Triathlon and she joined us at a remote broadcast. The little girl from Romania that you remember on the balance beam had grown into a lovely lady. I liked her personality as well. She was very friendly and upbeat.

We had a chance to visit about a lot of different topics. Nadia was living in Oklahoma with her husband, former U.S. gymnast Bart Conner. About an hour after the show, I got a call from Nadia's manager. Since I had recommended a few music venues for them to check out that evening, Nadia told her manager to invite me to hang with them. Normally I'd be tempted at such an offer, but Longhorn football had one of those 11 AM kickoffs the next day, which meant my pregame on-air duties began at 9 AM. There was no way I could go hang with Nadia and her manager for a night on the town. Yes, I can say (with some degree of honesty) that I turned down Nadia Comaneci.

## Ditka's Autograph

In 1996, I got a call from longtime Texas Rangers radio broadcaster Eric Nadel asking me if I'd like to work a few Sunday games that coming September. Since the Longhorns played football on Saturdays, I could hop a flight and be wherever I needed to be for the Rangers' game on Sunday. Of course, he didn't have to ask twice. One of the games was a Sunday afternoon contest in Anaheim against the California Angels.

Eric told me to make the arrangements through my travel agent and have the agency bill the Rangers. While on the phone with the agent, she suggested after the game I could have a 6-hour layover in Las Vegas, which would give me plenty of time to catch a cab, hit the strip, and make it back to the airport in time for the redeye to Austin. I liked that idea! After helping Eric call a 4-1 Rangers win, I caught a cab outside the ballpark for the Orange County airport and the flight to Vegas.

As I was waiting for the cab, I noticed former Phillies shortstop Larry Bowa standing just a few feet away. He was also waiting on a ride. At the time, Bowa was the Angels' third-base coach. It was a brief chat, but he thought it was cool that my partner for Longhorn baseball was his old teammate Keith Moreland, to whom he had given the nickname "Zonk" 18 years earlier. A couple of hours later I landed in Vegas. After a short shuttle ride to the strip, I walked into Bally's Casino and was immediately approached by a guy who clearly had been over-served. This is the way I remember the exchange.

"I can't believe it, it's Coach Ditka! I'm a huge fan. Would you mind signing an autograph, Coach?" He then hands me a crumpled-up piece of paper from his pocket.

"Sure, what is your name?"

"Joe, just make it out to Joe. Wow, this is so cool."

"Here you go, Joe. Have a great night, and be careful."

"Wow, thanks, Coach. This is great."

The next morning Joe woke up with a bad hangover and a fake autograph of Mike Ditka.

I've never been much of a casino guy, preferring the horse track. After unintentionally impersonating Ditka I made my way to a bar, played some video poker, and then tried my luck at the roulette wheel. One of my favorite baseball players when I was growing up was Richie "Dick" Allen, a slugger who had power to all fields. He wore #15, so I always tried to wear #15 when I played. That night, I just kept playing 15 at the roulette table.

On the fifth spin of the wheel, I had a hit. The payoff was around $250 so I called it a night and headed back to the airport with a couple of hours to spare. Adjacent to my gate there was a bar, so I figured I'd grab a nightcap which might help me sleep on the flight back to Austin. When I looked around the bar, I saw some forlorn folks. I'm sure a few of them had lost more than they had bargained for and were now about to head back to their respective cities a few dollars lighter.

"Hey, cheer up everybody," I yelled, "The next round is on me!" I had always wanted to do that. The bar tab was around $100, so I still cleared about $150. What a day! I got to call a major league baseball game, have a chat with Larry Bowa, win $250 at roulette, buy a round of drinks at a crowded bar, and sign an autograph as Mike Ditka. It was all in a day's work.

# Major

One of the most cerebral players I've had the pleasure to cover in my career is Texas Longhorn Quarterback Major Applewhite. After redshirting in 1997, the native of Baton Rouge was pressed into service early in the 1998 season because of an injury to starter Richard Walton. Even though he was undersized and not blessed with outstanding athletic ability, he had a knack for making big plays and was gritty, smart, tough, and a natural leader. He reminded me of a gym rat in basketball, like a point guard who knew how to run the offense, get the ball to his playmakers, always aware of the game situation.

An interview with Major was like a visit with a coach. I recall a postgame on-air chat when I asked him why a particular pass play worked. His response was nearly a minute long, as he recalled in vivid detail the location of every linebacker, safety and cornerback, the protection scheme and alignment, and the audible he called to counter what the defense was doing.

A few days before the 1999 Cotton Bowl (following the '98 season), Craig Way and I were broadcasting our afternoon talk show from the lobby of the team hotel, the Loews Anatole. Major stopped by to join us for a segment on his way to a dinner with his teammates. As we were wrapping up the chat, Major began fumbling with his tie. Apparently, the players were required to wear coats and ties to this function. Even though he was in his second year of college, it was quite evident that Major didn't know how to properly tie his tie. The final minute of the interview featured Craig and I giving the starting quarterback at the University of Texas an on-air lesson on how to fix his tie. I'm sure it was captivating radio.

Major went on to set 48 school records during his college career. In the Holiday Bowl following the 2001 season, Major was playing his last game and I was broadcasting my final football game at Texas. (I had already started with the Spurs a few months earlier) Major saved the best for last, as he led the Horns to a comeback win over the Washington Huskies. He set a school record with 473 passing yards and was named the Holiday Bowl MVP, capping off a career in which he went 22-8 as a starter.

It was only fitting that my last postgame guest that night was Major, who said, "I can see the headline in the *Austin American Statesman* tomorrow - 'Schoening and Applewhite Ride Off into the Sunset Together.'" I laughed at the notion but had to correct him, telling him his name should come first. After all, he had just set a school record for passing yards in a single game, and all I did was describe it. It didn't surprise anyone who knows Major that he went into coaching and is now an assistant at South Alabama.

# Lucchesi-Party of 10

On September 11th, 1999, the Longhorn football team traveled to Piscataway, New Jersey for an early-season nonconference matchup with the Scarlet Knights of Rutgers University. Since the Rutgers campus is just over an hour's drive from Philadelphia, each of my siblings and their spouses decided to make the short trip to North Jersey on Friday night, stay at a local hotel, and then enjoy the game on Saturday evening. My brother-in-law Joe Quattrone made the reservations for our party of ten at an upscale Italian restaurant called Alidante.

For the reservation, Joe gave the name "Lucchesi," which was the name of a notorious crime family from nearby New York City. Lucchesi was also the last name of my sister Liz's longtime boyfriend Salvatore, who would be with us that evening, but had no relation to the crime family whatsoever. Sal's family ran a fish store in the Italian Market in South Philly. We soon learned that having the name "Lucchesi" on our reservation would pay big dividends.

The owner of the establishment personally greeted our party, and assured us we would have a prime table "away from the windows." (You know, just in case of a drive-by.) We were seated immediately and were served complimentary bruschetta and wine before we even got totally settled in our chairs. I must say, it may have been the best service I've ever received in a restaurant. The owner checked on us several times to make sure the service, food, wine and ambiance were just right. We must've stayed there for over three hours grazing and drinking. From that point on, whenever my family made reservations at an Italian restaurant, it was under the name "Lucchesi."

## 69

## Inspirational No-hitter

On February 11th, 2000, my former team, Sam Houston State, was scheduled to play a nonconference baseball game at Disch Falk Field against the nationally-ranked Longhorns. Longtime SHSU head baseball coach John Skeeters asked me if I would take a few moments prior to the game and address his ballclub, and give them a bit of an inspirational speech. After batting practice and infield drills, Coach Skeeters assembled the players down the right-field line and I visited with them for about three minutes.

I told them about my background and how I had to fight through some adversity and overcame odds, etc. I then told them that I covered a Sam Houston State team that upset the powerful Oklahoma Sooners at Disch Falk in an NCAA Regional back in 1987. The players gave me a nice round of applause, Coach Skeeters thanked me, and I made my way up to the booth to broadcast the game.

Longhorn pitcher Beau Hale was a hard-throwing right-hander who was on top of his game that night. He had an excellent command of his breaking pitches and his fastball was nearly unhittable. That night, Hale recorded the first no-hitter in Big

XII Conference history. Incredibly, not one ball was hit to the outfield. There was one infield popup and 13 groundouts to go along with 13 strikeouts. In all my years of broadcasting baseball, it was the only no-hitter I had ever called.

The following night, Longhorn basketball coach Rick Barnes was in the studio for his weekly statewide radio show. Shortly after I opened the program, Barnes interrupted and told me I was barred from talking to members of his team. He looked serious. When I asked why he explained that anyone who was brought in to give an inspirational speech to a team that doesn't even get one hit is NOT going to talk to his players.

Although he was joking, Barnes reminded me of that "inspirational" speech whenever he got the chance. I totally deserved the ribbing. Hale, by the way, was selected by the Baltimore Orioles with the 14th pick of the first round of the 2000 amateur draft. He spent six years in the minors but never made it to the big leagues. In case you're wondering, I have not given a speech to any team since that February evening in Austin in 2000.

# 70

## How Far is Heaven?

Around 1996 I bought a cheap Ibanez guitar and started taking lessons, first from a guy named Roy Heinrich, and then from legendary Austin blues guitarist Van Wilks. I will admit upfront that I have never put in the time to become a good guitarist, but I was able to bang out some basic chords and form some melodies. I had always enjoyed writing (articles, columns, sportscasts, news and sports reports, poems, etc.) Now I decided I would try my hand at writing songs.

Many of the tunes I've written through the years were melodies that came to my mind while walking or swimming. I would record the tune on a tape recorder (later on an iPhone). Before I knew it, I had written a handful of tunes but was still a novice and a little shy about sharing them. I did mention during my talk show that I had begun this new venture. One evening I received an email from Austin-based music producer and bass player Joe Gracey, encouraging me to consider releasing a CD of my songs.

Joe had worked with Willie Nelson and was married to country singer/songwriter Kimmie Rhodes. Kimmie's son Gabe was a guitarist and aspiring producer and had a studio just behind their home. I agreed to give it a shot. Joe and Gabe helped me in all phases of putting together an eight-song CD, which I entitled "Life in the Minors." The CD Release party would be held at legendary Austin music venue The Saxon Pub. My three sisters, Peg, Liz, and Chris, surprised me by flying in from Philadelphia.

Also on the bill were The Groobees and Los Lonely Boys. The Groobees featured lead singer and songwriter Susan Gibson, who had penned "Wide Open Spaces," which became the Country Music Association's song of the year and a smash hit for The Dixie Chicks. Los Lonely Boys were relatively unknown in 2001, but a few years later they released "Heaven," which went straight to #1 on the Billboard charts. They have sold millions of albums and played huge stadiums and festivals through the years, but when I think of Los Lonely Boys I think of the night I opened the show for them in front of 150 people at the Saxon Pub.

My band that night included some very well-respected Austin musicians, including drummer Doug Robb, bassist Brad Kopp, guitarists T-Bird Jackson and Joel McColl and keyboard player Chip Dolan. These guys took the time to learn my songs, come to rehearsals and then play the gig. There was no money in it; these guys were just doing me a favor. The same cast of characters backed me up for a show in San Antonio about two years later. I don't play live shows very often, preferring to work in the studio with Nic Whitworth. I have now written or co-written over two dozen songs, and have released three CDs of original music. It's a fun hobby that has allowed me to explore my creative side.

*Sharing the bill with Los Lonely Boys before they made it big*

# 71

## "You're getting a call tonight"

In August of 2001, I was very excited about the upcoming Longhorn football season. Mack Brown was about to begin his fourth season. Brown was a master at recruiting, and some top freshmen would be complimenting returning veterans from a team that had gone 9-3 in 2000. One afternoon about a week before the season opener, station manager Lise Hudson called me into her office to tell me I would be getting a call at home that night from the program director at WOAI Radio in San Antonio. That's basically all she told me.

I knew that Jay Howard was the longtime play-by-play voice of the Spurs, and the only position at that station that would interest me at all would be the Spurs play-by-play gig. I took the call that evening from Andrew Ashwood, who was also known as the Gorilla, a guy with a big reputation in the radio business. He explained that the Spurs were thinking about making a change and convinced me to meet with him and some Spurs executives to discuss the position.

At the time, Gerry wasn't convinced it would be the best move. We had just built a beautiful home two years earlier, Eric was starting his senior year in High School and Karl was entering the fourth grade. Plus, Gerry had a very good position with the Texas Methodist Foundation in Austin. However, Eric convinced his mom that I should at least consider the move. The more I talked with WOAI and the Spurs, the more I was tempted to take the gig.

It would be NBA play-by-play plus a few daily reports on WOAI and The Ticket 760 in San Antonio. Power forward Tim Duncan was just about to enter his prime, and there would be an increase in salary. The most attractive part of the offer to me was the prospect of having the entire summer off. I had always wanted to travel but the two or three-week vacations in the summer were often centered around the need to see family back in the Philly/Jersey area. When the Spurs said it would be okay with them if I made the hour and a half commute from Austin for the games, I accepted the position.

UT Athletic Director DeLoss Dodds agreed to let me finish the Longhorn football season, and we were in business. On September 12th, 2001 (the day after 9/11) I signed a three-year contract to become the radio voice of the San Antonio Spurs. In the 21 seasons since, the Spurs have had the best winning percentage in the NBA, have won four championships, and I've had the chance to cover five Hall of Famers. (David Robinson, Tim Duncan, Gregg Popovich, Manu Ginobili and Tony Parker.) As of this writing, Parker, Ginobili and Pop have not yet been inducted, but it is only a matter of time.

Parker was the starting point guard for four title teams, won the 2007 Finals MVP Award, and spearheaded the resurgence of basketball in his native France. Ginobili is widely considered one of the best sixth men in the history of the NBA. He brought a passion to the game rarely seen before or since. His international credentials are off the charts, leading Argentina to amazing success in FIBA competitions and the Gold Medal in the 2004 Olympics in Athens. Pop has more wins than any coach in NBA history (regular season plus playoffs) and is one of only five coaches to win five NBA titles. So yes, accepting the Spurs' offer in 2001 turned out to be a pretty good move.

*Hanging with Brent Musburger and The Gorilla (Andrew Ashwood) before a playoff game in Dallas*

## Philly Billy

During my first season with the Spurs, I struck up a friendship with television analyst PJ Carlesimo, who would later become an assistant coach under Gregg Popovich. I was familiar with PJ since he had two previous stints as an NBA Head Coach (Golden State and Portland) and had nearly won an NCAA Championship as Head Coach at Seton Hall, a small Catholic University in South Orange, New Jersey. After finding out I was a native of the City of Brotherly Love, PJ dubbed me "Philly Billy."

At first, I wasn't crazy about the nickname, but that's what he insisted on calling me and soon it was picked up by several other staff members and players. Tim Duncan, Bruce Bowen, and Malik Rose (also a Philly native) all called me Philly Billy. To this day, Tim Duncan has never called me Bill, just "Philly." Carlesimo is also a native Pennsylvanian, hailing from the town of Scranton. Since he's been around the league so long in the capacity of television analyst, head coach, and assistant coach, he knows everybody, and everybody seems to know him.

In the preseason of 2003, we were in France for the NBA Global games and he invited me to attend a Catholic Mass at St. Roch's on the Rue St. Honoree' in Paris. The Mass was co-celebrated by a French priest and an American priest. The American, Father Connor, mentioned at the beginning of the service that he was from Pennsylvania. When the Mass concluded I approached the altar and introduced myself to Father Connor and asked where in Pennsylvania he lived.

When he said Scranton I told him the guy I was with was from Scranton. He looked out among the pews, and said, "Oh that's PJ Carlesimo, I know his entire family." He and PJ chatted for several minutes about the parishes of Scranton, and of various aunts, uncles and cousins in the Carlesimo clan. Even in the middle of Paris and nowhere near a basketball court, people still knew PJ Carlesimo.

PJ also is familiar with the best Italian restaurants in each NBA city. Early in my Spurs days, I would ask him for a recommendation. Not only did he tell me the name of the restaurant, he'd pass along the owner or manager's name and tell me to make sure I mentioned that he had sent me. That was excellent advice, because I would always get a good table, and usually a complimentary glass of wine or an appetizer. Thanks to PJ and his recommendations through the years, I'm fifteen pounds over my high school playing weight.

The nickname he gave me nearly two decades ago is still used by colleagues in the media. One day in the summer of 2008 while I was vacationing in Canada, Gerry and I were walking across the lobby of our hotel, and I heard "Philly Billy!" When I turned around it was the hotel clerk, who had checked us in the day earlier. He was smiling broadly. He then explained that he noticed my Spurs shirt the day before, and decided to do a Google search of my name to see if I was connected with the team. On my Wikipedia page, the nickname is mentioned. The clerk just wanted to make sure that it was me. Even though the internet, Google, and Wikipedia get the credit, I thought it was pretty funny that a complete stranger in another country was calling me by that nickname. Thanks, PJ!

---

For the past two decades, the San Antonio Spurs have embarked on the longest road trip of the season in February, because the San Antonio Livestock Show and Rodeo takes over the Spurs home arena, the AT&T Center. Through the years, I've written three songs about the trip, "8900 Miles," "It's February" and "Adios Auf Wiedersehen."

Because of my wanderlust, I always loved songs about the road. "Adios Auf Wiedersehen" is a nod to the Spurs international roster. While traveling with the Spurs in that era, any number of languages could be heard. It also didn't hurt that the Spurs had amazing success during these trips, as it usually built up momentum for the stretch run of the regular season.

---

*"Adios Auf Wiedersehen"*

*That time of year has come once again*

*We have to leave our family and friends*

*Make way for ropers and rodeo clowns*

*Livestock is here    We're leaving town*

*Chorus*

*Adios auf wiedersehen au revoir ciao*

*Nine straight road games    We'll get through somehow*

*No matter how you say it    We bid you adieu*

*Arrivederci    Sayonara too*

*We start in Minny    the forecast is snow*

*Then off to Motown    it's Hitsville ya know*

*Next stop is Brooklyn man we get around*

*Then Chicago    It's my kind of town*

*Repeat Chorus*

*Off to Cleveland   Rock and Roll Hall of Fame*

*Out to Sactown    get some sleep on the plane*

*The Clips in L.A. then Golden State*

*We wrap in Phoenix, let's celebrate*

*Repeat Chorus*

---

## 73

## Tony Senior

My first year in the NBA coincided with the rookie season for the Spurs' first-round draft pick that year, 19-year-old point guard Tony Parker of Paris Basket Racing in France. Tony was born in Belgium and grew up in France. His dad, Tony Parker Sr., a native of Chicago, played collegiately at Loyola University and then professionally in Europe. Young Tony was raw, slight, and untested, but was extremely quick and eager to learn.

Head Coach Gregg Popovich is not known for having a great deal of confidence in young players, but named Parker the starter less than two weeks into the season. Like any player that age, Parker had his share of ups and downs. Longtime San Antonio television personality Don Harris was hosting a show on Ticket 760 during afternoon drive. I was a guest one afternoon and Don was critical of Parker's recent play. I took the opportunity to defend Parker, reminding Harris that this guy is not even 20 years of age, has just arrived from another country, and he's running the point for a veteran ballclub with very high expectations.

About an hour later at my broadcast location in the Alamodome, a well-dressed gentleman approached me and asked if I was

Bill Schoening. When I said yes, he introduced himself as Tony Parker Sr. and informed me that he was listening to the talk show earlier when I defended his son. He told me that he appreciated it greatly and that I had a friend for life. I'd see Tony Sr. from time to time for the next few years, but we never got a chance to socialize very much. Then one night in 2006 he discovered I lived in Austin.

He asked me if I knew any of the music spots in town. Why, yes I believe I do! After that conversation, Tony Sr. would occasionally come to Austin for a music hang. We'd meet downtown and then proceed to blues clubs like Antone's or jazz clubs like the Elephant Room. Tony showed off his Chicago roots with the strong passion he showed for the music.

When the Spurs swept LeBron James and the Cleveland Cavaliers in the 2007 NBA Finals, two of the last folks remaining at the postgame party were Tony Parker Sr. and yours truly. It may have been his proudest moment. Just a few hours earlier, his son was named NBA Finals MVP. For me, I had just completed my 6th season in the NBA and the team I cover had won three titles. Yes, the wine that evening was French as I recall. Magnifique!

*Tony Parker Sr. loved coming up to Austin to check out the music scene*

## Manu Voodoo

I first heard of Manu Ginobili while perusing the Spurs media guide in 2001 shortly after I was hired. The Spurs had drafted the guard from Argentina late in the second round of the 1999 draft. He was playing for a team called Virtus Bologna in Italy. That season, Bologna won the Euroleague and Manu was named Euroleague Finals MVP. I remember thinking to myself that I'd love to see this guy play. Who knows, maybe he can come over and help the Spurs at some point.

The first time I got a chance to watch him was on television. He was playing for Argentina in the FIBA World games in the summer of '02, just a couple of months before he came to San Antonio. Ginobili led Argentina to the finals before a loss to Peja Stojakovic and the Yugoslavian National Team. I was impressed with his willingness to drive inside, his playmaking, and his leadership.

When Ginobili arrived, he added to the Spurs' growing international reputation, as he spoke fluent Spanish, Italian and English. His first game was in Los Angeles against the Lakers. At one point I saw him laughing as he came to the bench. I later asked him what was so funny. Manu explained, "Oh, that was just Kobe Bryant. He was trying to trash-talk me in Italian. His Italian is terrible."

As the season wore on, we saw flashes of brilliance as Manu came off the bench to provide a spark for the '02-03 championship team. There's no way I have enough room for all the Manu stories I want to tell. His on-court exploits alone are worthy of a book the length of War and Peace. I think one of the reasons he was so effective is because he understood angles and ways to attack using his left-hand drives.

He also perfected the euro-step, which is a legal move. The ball handler/driver takes a sideways step away from the defender to create a clearer lane to the goal. After the gather (when he picked up his dribble), Manu had a long stride and strong grip of the ball which allowed him to get close to the rim for a layup, dunk, or finger roll. He had all of these moves in his arsenal, plus he improved as a three-point shooter and developed a pull-up midrange jumper off the glass, and a floater from just inside the free-throw line. When he first nailed a three-pointer, I bellowed on the air, "That's a Manu Tres." I thought I'd throw a little Spanish into the broadcast in case he made one.

Ginobili retired with a franchise-record of 1,495 three-pointers made. Late in Ginobili's career, a fan came up to me before a game and said he wished he had a dollar for every time I said, "That's a Manu Tres." I told him he'd have over 1,400 dollars.

During the '04-05 season, I spent an off day at the race track, and when I mean off day, I mean off day. I was not working a game and my handicapping skills were not working either. I was down about $100 or so when I decided to bet the last race at Belmont Park in New York. I was actually in West Memphis, Arkansas at the Southland Greyhound Park, but was betting by simulcast. The #5 and the #10 horses were the ones to beat, but I liked the #1, a horse that had just been shipped in from Argentina. With respect for Manu Ginobili, I put the horse from

Argentina in my trifecta box. He won the race, nipping the #5 and #10 at the wire. The 1, 5, 10 trifecta paid $185, so I went from down $100 to up $85. I saved the race program and the next day I told Manu the story, showing him the #1 horse with (ARG) next to his name. Manu then asked me how much I won. I proudly told him $185. It was at that moment that I remembered that Manu had just signed a six-year, $52 million extension. I was bragging about winning what must have seemed like a minuscule amount.

Manu looked at the program, looked back at me, and said, "What is the word in English? Addiction! You have an addiction to these horses!" After practice in Indianapolis one day I stayed and watched one of the most entertaining games of H-O-R-S-E I had ever seen. Manu and teammate Brent Barry were trading shots and I was just soaking it all in. They were both making creative shots from all over the floor. At one point Ginobili went into the lane and bounced the ball off his head and into the basket. Barry protested vehemently, "None of this soccer shit is allowed!" Brent, by the way, wore a T-shirt on the plane one day that I loved. It was a horse shooting at a basket and below was spelled out   H U M A - .   Ya see, the horse was playing HUMAN.

Another time the Spurs had a game-day shootaround at the John Jay School of Criminal Justice in New York. It was much easier to have a light practice there than to try to navigate mid-morning Manhattan traffic to Madison Square Garden. After the shootaround, Bruce Bowen, Manu and I were the first three guys ready to leave the 4th-floor gym and head down to the bus. The team security officer told us the elevators would be packed because classes had just let out, and he directed us to a back stairway that would lead to the bus.

When we got to the bottom floor, there was a security camera and a huge sign. DO NOT EXIT HERE. THIS IS AN EMER-

GENCY EXIT ONLY. THE ALARM WILL SOUND. I thought the three of us were going to turn around and go back up the stairs, but Manu looked into the camera and said, "Hello my name is Manu Ginobili of the San Antonio Spurs. We just had a shootaround in the gym. We are not stealing anything, but we are leaving." As we exited those doors, a loud siren could be heard blaring throughout midtown Manhattan.

Bruce, Manu and I laughed all the way to the bus. As far as I know, the authorities never tracked down Manu. He was easy enough to find. He played in front of 20,000 fans that night at Madison Square Garden. I must say the highlight of my career is calling every NBA game Manu Ginobili played. From the preseason through the playoffs, if Manu put that #20 jersey on home or away, I was there. It was heartwarming to see fans from Argentina who made their way to Spurs games just for a chance to catch a glimpse of their hero.

He always obliged the fans after his warm-up routine. He would pose for pictures, sign autographs, and shake hands. The night after Cardinal Jorge Bergoglio was elected to the papacy (Pope Francis) I kidded with Manu that he would no longer be the most popular person in Argentina. "I think now I am third- the Pope is first, Diego Maradona (soccer star) is second, and I am third, and that's okay with me." By the way, Ginobili posted a winning percentage of .721 during his 16 seasons with the Spurs and that is the best in the history of the NBA among players who have appeared in at least 1,000 games.

*Guard Manu Ginobili played with a ferocity and determination that endeared him to fans from San Antonio to Buenos Aires*

# Jimmy Chang

During the '02-03 season, the Spurs signed a 7-foot center from Mongolia named Mengke Bateer, who had played the previous season with the Denver Nuggets. Bateer spoke very little English so the Spurs hired a young Chinese-American from California named Jimmy Chang to be his translator. Bateer didn't play much, but Chang was on every road trip, and he especially enjoyed the fine food served on the charter flights.

Chang was fun - a jovial, heavyset guy with a sarcastic sense of humor. He also followed sports very closely. Late in the season, on an off day in Boston, the Spurs practiced at a local college. I was urged by several staffers to get ready for a one-on-one challenge vs. Jimmy Chang. I was not ready to play. I was wearing a pair of jeans and a button-down shirt, but apparently, Steve Kerr and Danny Ferry had a little wager on this epic battle, and the game was on. I was horrible. I was out of shape, hadn't touched a ball in years, and I had just eaten lunch.

Jimmy was much younger but probably weighed close to 300 pounds. Many of the players observed the game from courtside bleachers. Head Coach Greg Popovich watched from a folding chair near midcourt. As Jimmy and I huffed and puffed through several minutes of missed shots and loose rebounds, we found ourselves tied at 2 baskets apiece when Pop announced that whoever scores next would win the game. I looked up above the court and Manu Ginobili, who had hit the showers after practice, was now watching wearing only a towel.

Jimmy started a drive with his head lowered, so I beat him to the spot and he barreled into me as he threw a shot up off the backboard. The shot went in. Ferry jumped up to say the basket was good but Kerr was saying, "Wave it off - offensive foul." Arguments ensued. Apparently, $50 was riding on this! As for me, I was watching the proceedings from the floor of the gym, trapped beneath the Great Wall of China, I mean Jimmy Chang. I don't know that I have ever seen Pop laugh so hard. At this point, Pop declared the game a 2-2 draw, and the fun was over for the day. I've run into Jimmy Chang several times through the years, and he always says "block" and I always say "charge."

# Lambeau

During my early days with the Spurs, I was offered the chance to broadcast a few NFL games for an outfit called the Jones Radio Network. I was working in the NBA, had already worked some major league baseball games and now I had the chance to complete the major professional sports trifecta. My favorite assignment was a game featuring the New York Giants at Green Bay. I actually was going to get a chance to call a game from the legendary Lambeau Field! It wasn't exactly the Frozen Tundra, however. It was a bright and warm September afternoon.

I don't remember much about that game, but I do recall not being able to book a flight back to Austin that evening, so I had dinner by myself at Brett Favre's restaurant (Brett wasn't there) and flew back on Monday morning. Since there are very few direct flights out of Green Bay, I caught a "puddle jumper" to Chicago, where I would catch my connecting flight home. Next to me on the initial flight was a heavy-set New Yorker, proudly wearing his blue Jeremy Shockey Giants jersey.

I asked him how his Lambeau Field experience went, and I'll always remember his response, which came in a very thick New

York accent, "It was awesome. These people here are so friendly. Before the game, I'm walking through the parking lot, with my Giant's jersey on, and I was invited to eat bratwurst and drink beers. A couple of weeks ago in Philadelphia, I did not get that same kind of reception."

# Beno

In 2004, the Spurs drafted a 21-year-old point guard named Beno Udrih. The lefty from Slovenia spoke pretty good English and had a funny sense of humor. One time I was joking with him because he was one of the few players on the team that was an eligible bachelor. I asked him if he had a "little black book" for his social life. He laughed and said, "No, I have a BIG black book." After a road win in Atlanta, Beno was our "impact player of the game". He joined me live courtside for a brief post game conversation.

When I told Beno I liked his fifteen-foot pull-up jumper, he agreed that perhaps he should shoot it more. "Like on that fast break I had with Devin Brown," he explained, "I should've taken shot. Instead, I pass the ball to Devin and make a turnover. I f*ck up." This was on live radio. The producer back at the station didn't catch it, so it made the airwaves. I quickly changed the subject and continued the interview as if nothing had happened.

After I got off the air, I received a text from my son Eric. "Did Beno just say what I thought he said?" Well, yes he did. Before boarding the plane, I saw Beno and told him he can say "messed" up or "screwed" up. In the rear of the plane back to San Antonio, I told the story to Spurs athletic trainer Will Sevening, who had a brainstorm. Will had the responsibility of placing "Fine Slips" in a player's locker if that player had been fined by the NBA. He had actual fine slips in his backpack.

Will then asked me how much we should "fine" Beno for cursing on the radio. We agreed that $1,000 would be a good amount. The next night, Beno was greeted by that fine slip in his locker. He approached Sevening about the fine and said, "I said curse word to Philly Billy on radio, and now I get fined $1,000 American." Will had some fun at Beno's expense but eventually told him the fine wasn't real. Beno played 13 seasons in the NBA for 8 different teams. I ran into him often, but I never let him forget the F-Bomb he dropped on the air in Atlanta during his rookie season.

## The Spurs Melting Pot

Since I always had a curiosity about language, history, and geography, the NBA was a great place to be in the early 2000s. The league was starting to draft and develop an increasing number of players from all over the globe. By my third season with the Spurs, four of the top five scorers on the team were from Europe or South America. The Spurs were ahead of the curve when it came to international scouting. Through the years, I have come to appreciate these players and their backgrounds. Their backstories are interesting as well.

In my 21 seasons with the Spurs, we have had Manu, Mengke, Hedo, Rasho, Beno, Francisco, Fabricio, Tiago, Nando, Boris, Marco, Boban, Pau, Nico, Joffrey, Demo, Marco and Luka. I've always made an attempt to reach out to these players when they first arrived to hear about where they are from and how their upbringing shaped them as people, not just basketball players. Our Spanish radio play-by-play announcer is Paul "Publio" Castro, who has been with the team for 27 years.

Before a preseason game with a Greek team called Panathinaikos, Publio needed help pronouncing the name of a guard. I remembered this player from his previous NBA days. His name was Sarunas Jasikevicius (pronounced Yas a KEV a chis). When Publio tried to say it came out, "yes, we have cabbages." After the game, I asked him how it went, "Guess who had 16 points?" he bragged, "Yes, we have cabbages!"

In October of 2014, the Spurs played Fehnerbache Ulker of Istanbul, a perennial power in the Turkish League. One look at their roster and I knew I had a challenge on my hands. So I wrote a little reggae beat and then pronounced their names while singing the melody. I called it "Ballers from Istanbul." I think it actually helped me pronounce the names of players like Nemanja Bjelica, Melih Mahmutoglo, and Emir Preldzic. I'm not certain, but it may be the only reggae song ever written about a Turkish Basketball team.

---

When one is about to call a sporting event featuring players from all over the world, the pronunciation guide is a very valuable tool. I haven't written many novelty songs, but this one may qualify.

---

*"Ballers from Istanbul"*

*Nemanja Bjelica Melih Mahmutoglu Izzet Turkyilmaz just to name a few*

*Luka Zoric  Berk Ugurlu Kenan Sapahi  He's good too*

*Chorus*

*This is the best way I know how*

*To say these foreign names when they commit a foul*

*Emir Preldzic Serhat Ceten Semih Erden will it never end?*

*Oguz Savas Jan Vessley too  Can Altinting  Yeah this is quite a crew*

*Repeat Chorus*

*Repeat First Verse*

## What's Your Title again?

In October of 2009, the Spurs traveled to Bloomington, Indiana to play a preseason game against the Indiana Pacers. When I was broadcasting college games, I never got the opportunity to broadcast a game at Assembly Hall, home of the Hoosiers. Years ago, NBA teams would often play preseason games in non NBA cities, so here was my chance to call a game in a storied college gym. As always, I got to the arena several hours before tipoff. At the end of the bench to my left, I saw the very familiar face of Hall of Famer Larry Bird. At the time, Bird was serving as the Pacers President of Basketball Operations.

Since there was nobody else around and it was so early, I thought I'd ask him if he'd give me two minutes for a pregame interview. I introduced myself, and he said yes, and invited me to sit down next to him. I wasn't quite sure what his title was at the time, so before we started the interview, I asked him if he was President of Basketball Operations or General Manager. He looked at me and smirked, "I don't know, you can call me whatever you want, I'm just the head asshole in charge."

## 80

## Red Rocket

On June 21st, 2006, The Spurs traded center Rasho Nesterovic to the Toronto Raptors for forwards Matt Bonner and Eric Williams and a second-round draft choice. Shortly after the trade was official, I got a phone call from the television voice of the Raptors Chuck Swirsky. I'd known Chuck since my early Longhorn days when he was the voice of the DePaul Blue Demons. Chuck called to tell me that I would get along great with Bonner. He was right on the mark with that prediction.

For nine years, Matt was a joy, always cooperative with the media, and usually good for a laugh or two during the interview. His folksy, self-deprecating humor was endearing, but this guy could also play. He shot 41% from three-point range during his Spurs career and ranks fifth all-time in franchise history for 3 pointers made. Every once in a while, he would fake a three, drive the ball inside, use a jump stop in the middle of the lane, and swish an eight-foot face up hook shot. That's when I would bellow on air, "Kareem Abdul JaBonner!" Bonner's hook shot looked absolutely nothing like Kareem's but that was sort of the point.

Like some folks from New England, Matt would often put the word "wicked" before an adjective. If I asked him how he was doing that particular day, he'd respond "wicked awesome." That expression is now part of my everyday jargon. For a while Matt wrote a blog on the Spurs website called "The Sandwich Hunter,: as he made his way through the NBA, dining on all different types of sandwiches.

In December of '09, the Spurs were scheduled to play a game against the Utah Jazz in Salt Lake City. My son Eric had lived in Salt Lake since 2007, and was familiar with a place where we could enjoy an authentic Philly Cheesesteak. "Moochie's" was owned by Joann Renzi, a lady who grew up in the Kingsessing section in my neighborhood of Southwest Philly. Matt met up with us in the lobby, and we made the chilly ten-minute walk from the team hotel.

At first, Matt was hesitant about eating a heavy meal like a cheesesteak on a game day, but he ordered one with onions and peppers. He thoroughly enjoyed his lunch, but how would his stomach hold up? About seven hours later, Matt took the floor for the Spurs and rarely looked better. He connected on 10 of 14 shots from the field, including 4 three-pointers. The Spurs, however, came up on the short end of a 104-101 score. During his NBA career, Matt Bonner played 792 regular-season games and 94 playoff games, but his best scoring night ever came on December 7th, 2009, when he tallied 28 points at Utah after digesting a Philly Cheesesteak from Moochie's. Yes, I still take full credit.

*A postgame visit with the Red Rocket*

## Chillin' at Churchill

I'm so fortunate that on several occasions in my life I've been able to turn a negative into a positive. One such time was in 2011. The top-seeded Spurs suffered a first-round loss at the hands of the Memphis Grizzlies, and suddenly, the season came to a halt on April 29th. Very rarely am I free on the first Saturday in May, but that was going to be the case in 2011.

Since my dad got me into horse racing, one of the items on my bucket list was to attend the Kentucky Derby, which is held the first Saturday in May. On a whim, I called my old friend Paul Rogers, the longtime voice of the University of Louisville Cardinals. I just wanted to inquire about the chance of getting a media credential. He told me he'd get right back to me. Within ten minutes, he returned the call and said I had a press pass for the entire weekend, a room at his house (if I wanted to stay there) and an invitation to Rick Pitino's party the night before the race. I just needed to make my way to Louisville. Paul hooked me up – I was excited.

Flights in and out of Louisville were completely booked so I flew into Cincinnati, which is only 100 miles away. Since Paul was broadcasting his morning program from a remote studio at

Churchill Downs, I was able to stand along the rail and watch the Derby horses go through their early morning workouts. I had been going to the track since I was a 12-year-old kid, but I had never seen horses that looked like this. These derby horses were sleek, shiny, muscular and carried themselves with an air of confidence. It was almost like each of these horses knew he was worth $1 million or more.

Kentucky Oaks Day is on Friday, and my media credential gave me carte blanche. I had a spot to watch all the races in the press box, but I didn't stay there the entire time. I went next door to "Millionaire's Row." I had never seen so many pretty ladies with large floppy hats in my entire life. The men were decked out in suits and ties as well. There was a lot of seersucker on display. Just above the bar, there was a large monitor and as I was getting ready to watch the next race, the bartender handed me a Mint Julep. I guess he thought I was one of the millionaires. Needless to say, I watched a few races in that comfortable and cozy environment.

I may not be a millionaire, but that day I sure felt like one. That evening Paul and I made our way to the YUM Center, the basketball arena for the Louisville Cardinals, where Coach Pitino was hosting his soiree. It was great to meet Coach Pitino that evening and to sip on the complimentary Italian wine. Among the guests was CBS broadcaster Lesley Visser, and we shared a laugh about the Greensboro incident that had occurred 19 years earlier. (That was when my producer Kent Koen talked about how good-looking Lesley was while completely unaware that she was listening in.)

The next day was Derby Day, almost a carbon copy of Friday. Pretty horses, ladies, hats, and outfits, a few handicapping wins and a few losses, and some good laughs. I remember spending part of the day with ESPN anchor Kenny Mayne, who had a dry but funny sense of humor. There was a crowd of over 137,000 that day, but I had plenty of room in the press box, plus a betting window nearby and of course- Millionaire's Row! Yes, I went back for an encore! I did not pick the winner of the race that day (Animal Kingdom) but I ended up having one of the best weekends of my life, thanks to my old friend Paul Rogers, who is still the radio voice of the Louisville Cardinals.

*My wife actually asked me to find some pretty ladies with hats at the Derby. Apparently, some of her co-workers wanted to get a sense of the fashion on display. I didn't have to look far.*

---

It took me a while to realize that most of the problems I have encountered in this life were due to my own poor decisions and mistakes. Like many folks, I sometimes blamed others for my missteps. This wasn't a healthy philosophy because it could potentially damage relationships and shift the focus of the issue away from the main culprit - myself! Once I became less centered on me and more focused on God, it was easier for me to deal with life's everyday challenges, and appreciate the beauty and wonder around me. That was my mindset when I wrote "Most of My Pain."

---

*"Most of My Pain"*

*Most of my wounds are self inflicted*

*A lot my pain at my own hand*

*Most of my lies had consequences*

*A lot of my tears fell on the land*

*Chorus*

*You opened up my heart*

*Gave me reason to sing*

*Now I know my part*

*To see you in everything*

*Most of my time I lack direction*

*A lot of my path on my own terms*

*Most of my fears*

*they were unfounded*

*A lot of lessons were hard to learn*

*Repeat chorus*

---

## Blame it on Springsteen

During the 2016-17 NBA preseason, Bruce Springsteen released his epic autobiography "Born to Run," named after his iconic 1975 Columbia album that turned a Jersey shore kid with a Telecaster into a rock star. I had planned on purchasing the book, but at the time I was reading another book about Satchel Paige, the famous Negro League pitcher.

I have very strange reading habits when it comes to books. I can never read two at the same time. Even if it takes me a month or two to finish a book, I won't start another until the current one is finished. Anyway, for Christmas my son Eric presented me with a copy of "Born to Run." At 528 pages, it would be the longest book I would ever read (No, I did not read "War and Peace"). By the time the annual Spurs Rodeo Road Trip commenced in February, I was making excellent progress on the book. On the night of February 12th, we were on our way to Indianapolis for a game with the Indiana Pacers.

As we were landing, I was reading Springsteen's account of the final days of his longtime organist Danny Federici. In the book, Springsteen mentioned that Danny's last gig with the E Street Band was at Conseco Field House in Indianapolis. Suffering from melanoma, Federici played only portions of that show and died a month later. I thought it was a bit ironic that I had been reading the part about Danny's final gig being in Indianapolis as we were making our final approach into that city.

The following night, as I opened the live radio broadcast, I said, "Good evening and welcome to Conseco Fieldhouse in Indianapolis." I then went on for a few moments, finished my opening segment, and pitched it back to the studio. My longtime producer Mike Bartlett, who has saved my butt on several occasions, asked me during the commercial break why I was calling the arena Conseco Field House when it had been known as Bankers Life Field House for the past five years.

It then occurred to me that when I wrote my intro for the game it was shortly after we landed, and the Springsteen/Federici/Conseco reference was still on my mind. I told Mike that Springsteen was to blame. This was all Bruce's fault! I explained the situation to him. Not convinced, and unimpressed, Mike then informed me that on my taped pregame interview with guard Patty Mills, I called it Conseco again! Damn it, Bruce, you're killing me over here. Mike said not to worry, and he edited the "Conseco" out of the interview. The on-air version became, "We're joined by Patty Mills at the Fieldhouse." In the big scheme of things, it's really not that big a deal, but it has become a running joke that if something goes wrong technically, or if an incorrect sponsor or arena name gets mentioned, we just blame it on Springsteen.

## 83

## This place gives me the creeps

On March 22nd, 2014, the Spurs were playing a road back-to-back with the Sacramento Kings and the Golden State Warriors. In the NBA, the term "back-to-back" simply means games are played on successive nights. After a 99-79 win over the Kings, we headed to the Bay Area to play the Warriors, who played their home games in Oakland. We normally would stay in San Francisco, but since we didn't have much time there, it was decided we would stay at the Claremont Club and Spa in Berkeley.

Opened in 1915, the Claremont is a stately structure with gorgeous views of the city across the bay. Paul "Publio" Castro, who has called Spanish radio play-by-play for the Spurs since the early '90s, was with me. After checking in with the team, we took the elevator and then walked down the hall to our rooms, which were about 30 feet apart on the fourth floor. I distinctly remember thinking that the long narrow hallway reminded me of "The Shining", which starred Jack Nicholson as a murderous psychopath.

As I unpacked my bag I started hearing a strange sound. It was a combination of a high-pitched wind and pipes creaking. It was hard to tell from which direction the sound was coming, but it continued. At that moment I was startled by my cell phone dinging. It was Publio texting me to say that the Claremont Hotel was giving him the creeps. I was feeling the exact same way.

He then asked if I had heard the kids playing with a ball in the hallway. I had not, so I opened the door and looked down the long, narrow hallway (which was now REALLY starting to look like the hallway in "The Shining"), but there were no kids. I assured Publio that there the hallway was clear and that we should both ignore these sounds and try to get some sleep. It took me longer to doze off than normal, but without further incident, I fell asleep around 2 am. When I stopped in the gift shop the next morning, the clerk was very cheery and upbeat. When she inquired if I had slept well, I shared with her that I was hearing strange noises and my friend a few doors down heard kids in the hallway after 1 am.

Her response was very casual. "Oh, you must be up on the fourth floor, right?" When I responded that I was indeed, and staying in Room 423, she laughed. "Well, that little girl is in 422." When I asked about the little girl, she handed me a brochure about the history of hauntings at the Claremont. In the early days of the hotel, laundry chutes were used by housekeeping to throw used sheets and towels down to the basement to be washed. One day, a six-year-old girl followed her bouncing ball into a laundry chute and fell to her death. From that day on, guests have heard kids playing and balls bouncing, especially on the fourth floor. There are some folks that are really into ghosts who make a sojourn to the Claremont and request to stay in Room 422.

It's my guess that the Spurs won't be staying at the Claremont anytime soon. Assistant Coach Ime Udoka (now the head coach of the Boston Celtics) told me the place freaked him out, and forward Jeff Ayres couldn't open his door when he got to his assigned room and then heard a baby crying in that room. When he went to the front desk to tell them a mistake had been made, the clerk called the room and there was no answer. She double-checked the rooming list and Jeff's room definitely had not been rented and was not occupied. He was offered a different room, and he quickly accepted. I've never been one to believe in ghosts, but there's some strange stuff going on at the Claremont Resort and Spa in Berkeley, California.

## 84

## "That's how ya got it"

One of the most colorful yet controversial game officials in NBA history is Joe Crawford, a native of Havertown, a suburb just west of Philadelphia. In his NBA career, Crawford worked a record 374 playoff games. He worked in the NBA from 1977-2016. Crawford was known for his take-charge approach and his willingness to assess players or coaches a technical foul. I first saw Joe Crawford referee a basketball game in 1975, when he was working the 6'5 and under league at McCreesh playground.

While I ran the clock or kept the scorebook, Joe Crawford was the official, making calls in a demonstrative style that we would sometimes emulate. A traveling call would prompt Joe into a hop, skip, and a jump while he blew his whistle, "I got steps - we're goin' this way." If you pushed off to get a rebound, he would bellow, "Nah nah, that's how you got it!" Crawford attended Cardinal O'Hara High School, which was in the Catholic League South Division, the same division as my alma mater, West Catholic.

In 2003, twenty-eight years after we both worked in that outdoor recreation league, Joe was the lead official in a western conference semifinal series. He spotted me broadcasting courtside before the Spurs tipped off against the Lakers at Staples Center. Just a few minutes before tip, he trotted over to my broadcast location. He pointed at me and yelled, "Are you on the air?" I said no, as I was in my final commercial break. He then scowled at me as if he was angry and concluded, "Well, I just wanted to tell you something…When I was at O'Hara, we kicked the shit out of West Catholic!"

He then turned toward center court, where moments later he threw the ball up between Shaquille O'Neal and Tim Duncan. We had both come a long way from McCreesh Playground. Although he was a take-charge and no-nonsense official that was not liked by everybody, I enjoyed watching Crawford work, and always thought he was one of the best officials in the league.

## Redemption Season

The most difficult loss I can recall in my four decades of describing games came in game 6 of the NBA finals in 2013. The Spurs were up three games to two and had a five-point lead with 28 seconds remaining. The championship was in their grasp. A number of unlikely occurrences resulted in sharpshooter Ray Allen getting a good look for a corner three-pointer that tied the game and forced overtime. The Heat went on to win Game 6 and then edged the Spurs in Game 7.

The Spurs could have retooled and revamped in 2014, but with very few changes, and with a grim determination, the 2013-14 Spurs were on a mission from day one. They won 14 of their first 16 games and finished with a 62-20 overall record, the best in the NBA. A tough first-round test provided by the Dallas Mavericks got the Spurs going. They dispatched Portland in five games and outlasted a tough Oklahoma City team in six games to reach the finals against the team they wanted to face all along, LeBron James, Dwayne Wade, Chris Bosh, and the defending champion Miami Heat.

What followed was the best team basketball these eyes have ever witnessed. Exquisite ball movement, hard screens, backdoor cuts, and a steely focus were all on display, as the Spurs won the series four games to one, with an average margin of victory of 18 points. The Spurs shot an NBA finals record 54 percent from the floor. The 2014 NBA season and championship will always go down as my favorite, simply because it was built from the ashes of a bitter disappointment the year before.

## Iceman

One of the cool aspects of working for the Spurs has been the chance to get to know a few of the legendary players who have played for the organization, especially Hall of Famer George "The Iceman" Gervin, who is known affectionately as "Ice". After leading the NBA in scoring four times, and being named to the NBA all-star team nine times, Ice retired and stayed in San Antonio, where he started an academy for youngsters and stayed actively involved in the community.

I've had the chance to interview Ice at a number of Spurs functions, and have always enjoyed his laid-back approach to life. His nickname fits his persona perfectly because he is simply one of the coolest cats ever. One of the Spurs sponsors, the KIA Motor Company, wanted to do something special for their employees so they formed two basketball teams, one would consist of folks who worked in sales and marketing, and the other team featured employees who worked in the service department.

For several years, they staged an annual game played on the floor at the AT&T Center. I was asked to serve as Head Coach a few times, and one year the opposing coach was the Iceman. Even though it was a fun afternoon, there were competitive juices flowing. I had my team employ a 2-3 zone, but that strategy was ineffective as Ice's team hit some three-pointers down the stretch and Team Gervin edged Team Schoening. I was kiddingly trying to trash talk Ice during the game, but he just laughed it off in typical Ice fashion.

Whenever we would travel internationally for the NBA Global Games, the league made sure that Ice came along as an Ambassador. One time in Mexico City, I bumped into Ice at the team hotel, and he informed me that he was serving in his "ambassador role." I asked him if that meant he was going to shake hands, sign autographs, and kiss babies. He just smiled and said, "That's what the Iceman do."

In 2014 when the Spurs played preseason games in Berlin and Istanbul, the chartered plane needed to stop for refueling at the Reykjavik Airport in Iceland. It resulted in about an hour layover. As we stretched our legs in the airport at 3 AM waiting to board the plane for the final leg back to San Antonio, Spurs television analyst Sean Elliott pointed out Ice standing by himself near the gate. I knew what I had to do. Although I already had several photos with him, I couldn't resist. Yes, I got a picture taken with The Iceman in Iceland. How many people can say that?

*The Iceman in Iceland*

# Boban

Prior to the 2015-16 season, the Spurs signed a very intriguing prospect. At 7'4" and 295 pounds, Serbian Center Boban Marjanovic was an all Euroleague first-teamer and was a three-time MVP of the Serbian Super League. He was the tallest player I had ever covered and may have also been the friendliest. He consistently had a warm smile and instantly became a crowd favorite at the AT&T Center. In a preseason game, he caught the ball under the basket, and with his feet barely leaving the floor, he just slammed it down. I have no idea why, but I blurted out "From Serbia, With Love!"

I asked Boban the next day if the new expression was okay with him. He told me that he liked it a great deal. It became a staple whenever he dunked. Spurs fan Jane Craig even made a poster with Boban's likeness next to big bold letters, "From Serbia With Love." She flashed that sign whenever Boban slammed one home. If he didn't have to worry about the three-second violation in the lane on offense and defense, he would have been a dominant force.

Boban enjoyed doing interviews, but would always apologize for his English, which was actually not bad at all. On an early-season road trip to Portland, I was dining alone at an Italian restaurant called Pazzo. I was just about to pay the bill when Boban and guard Ray McCallum stopped by to say hello. They had just concluded their meal and invited me to join them for dessert at a nearby Baskin Robbins. Walking the block to the ice cream shop was an adventure. Nearly every person we passed stopped and stared at this massive, imposing figure.

Although Boban was well aware that folks were gawking, he took it all in stride. He was used to people staring at him. When we walked into the Baskin Robbins, the server behind the counter was a short fellow who was busy wiping down the counter before he looked up at his new customers. I watched as, almost in slow motion, he moved his head up higher and higher in wide-eyed amazement before finally seeing Boban's face. Before asking what he wanted to order, he blurted out, "Exactly how tall are you?" Without hesitation, Boban responded, "This is question I never get."

Following his one season with the Spurs, Boban signed a three-year deal with the Detroit Pistons worth $21 million. When the Spurs played the Pistons in a preseason game a few months later, I interviewed Boban for our pregame show. I had to wait a while as many of his former teammates and coaches wanted to visit with him as well. During the interview, he told me he felt bad about leaving the Spurs, but that head coach Gregg Popovich had encouraged him to sign with the Pistons since the Spurs did not have the available funds to match the Pistons offer.

Boban also said that there was a strong Serbian presence in the metro area of Detroit, but that wasn't necessarily good for him because he wanted to improve his English and his conditioning, but the native Serbians wanted to speak in their language and constantly feed him dishes from the old country. At the end of the interview, I told Boban how much I missed him being around, and he responded, "Bill, I have for you much affection." The feeling was mutual.

*Everybody loves Boban*

# Epinal

In the spring of 2013, I reconnected with Kelly Bostrom. Kelly was one of the top radio, television and film students at Sam Houston State when I hired her as a part-time assistant in the KSAM News department. My confidence in Kelly and her abilities as both a reporter and anchor allowed me to accept the offer to call Texas A&M baseball games in the spring of 1989.

Shortly after graduating from SHSU, Kelly was hired as a news reporter at KBTX TV in Bryan/College Station. While she was there, she met Bernard Robic, a Frenchman who was teaching an evening class at Texas A&M. They fell in love, married, and moved to several places before they settled in Thomery, a charming village of 3500, located along the Seine River about 50 miles south of Paris.

It was during the Spurs playoff run of 2013 when Kelly (who was in Texas for vacation) asked me to meet her and her mom for lunch. It was during that lunch that Kelly invited me to visit Thomery. I had already been to Paris twice and was planning to take my sister Liz on an August trip to Rome. Gerry suggested that we just extend our trip a few days, and go visit Kelly.

Then Gerry mentioned my Uncle Thomas, who is buried at the U.S. Military Cemetery in Epinal, in the Vosges Mountains of Eastern France. I had often talked of visiting the grave of my father's younger brother, who was killed in action on January 19th, 1945 at Herrlisheim, a French town on the Rhine River. Kelly explained that there were no bus lines or trains to the Cemetery at Epinal, so she offered to make the eight-hour round trip drive. To this day, it remains one of the biggest favors anyone has done for me. This was finally my chance to visit Uncle Thomas.

When we arrived at the cemetery, we had come prepared with his purple heart and a 1944 US Army photo, taken just before he shipped overseas. The cemetery caretaker, Karine Nederlander, was also prepared. She had umbrellas (since it was a rainy day), a French and a U.S. flag, and a bucket of sand from the beaches at Normandy. There are 5,000 Americans at Epinal but Karine knew exactly where Uncle Thomas was. When we stopped at the grave, Karine took the sand and rubbed the indentations of the marble cross so the name could be read clearly.

Thomas F Schoening

PFC 119 Engineer Battalion 12th Armored Division

Pennsylvania Jan. 19, 1945

When the name Schoening became evident because of the sand, I started weeping, but not for me; the tears were for my late dad. He loved his younger brother dearly but rarely talked about him. I think the pain was just too much to bear. I learned a lot about Uncle Thomas and WWII from my mom, who kept two thick scrapbooks about the war. One book chronicled the Pacific War and the other followed the European theater. Family photos, military portraits, newspaper and magazine articles filled the books.

She also kept the letter from the war department expressing sympathy to the family. My tears at Epinal continued to flow as I thought of my grandparents, who made the difficult decision to have Thomas buried at Epinal with his comrades. Many of these servicemen and women had been killed during the Battle of the Bulge, the last German offensive of the war.

I thought how ironic it must've been for my grandfather, who was a first-generation American. His father Rudolf emigrated to the U.S. from Hamburg in 1882. I thought of the Uncle I never knew and the fact that he had so much life in front of him. Then I looked out over that beautiful green pasture and saw the countless rows of crosses. All of those brave men and women never made it home. It was at that moment, time really did seem to stand still.

*From privates to generals*
*Every rank between*
*Honored in this field*
*Tuskegee airmen and infantry*
*At their graves I kneel*

I wrote those words on the plane back to the States from Paris. When I returned, I enlisted the help of my good friends Mike Vasquez and Stephen Doster, both excellent guitarists. Nic Whitworth produced the song and provided keyboards, while Melissa Jacks played a haunting flute solo after the second verse. Another friend, videographer Rod Henegar found WWII archival footage and pictures from Epinal and put together a video. I've written over two dozen songs, but "Tears at Epinal" will likely always be the most emotional.

256 • STORIES, SPORTS, AND SONGS

*An emotional day with sister Liz at the grave of Uncle Thomas.*

*Uncle Thomas*

---

Growing up with a dad who had experienced so much during World War II had an effect on me. I developed a deep interest in that major event in human history. To this day, it's hard to imagine that it was my father's generation that had to confront and stop such evil. For many younger folks, WWII is something that happened in the previous century, but for me it hit much closer to home.

---

***"Tears at Epinal"***

*5,000 crosses all lined in rows deep in eastern France*

*Mark the resting places of young heroes*

*Who never really had a chance*

*Chorus*

*The sky cries   Time stands still*

*For those who answered the call*

*The guns have been silent for 68 years*

*But there are tears at Epinal*

*My Uncle Thomas was just 19 when he shipped overseas*

*Sent to the lines   Battle of the Bulge*

*A landmine ended his dreams*

*Repeat Chorus*

*From privates to generals   Every rank between*

*Honored in this field   Tuskegee airmen and infantry*

*At their graves I kneel*

*Repeat Chorus*

---

## Ego deflation

I'll never forget how excited I was when I found out I would be receiving a 2003 NBA Championship ring. I had covered some teams that won a district or conference title but never a national championship of any kind. Here I was, in just my second year in the Spurs organization, and I'm already getting sized up for a ring. Although I thought the Spurs had a bright future with some young talent, I never dared dream that the Spurs would win three more championships with me at the radio microphone.

As I accumulated rings, I passed them down. The '03 ring now belongs to my older son Eric, the '05 ring is my younger son Karl's, and my wife Gerry got the '07 ring. I will likely never give up the '14 ring because it reminds me of my favorite season ever. On occasion, I'll wear the '14 ring, which is just a tad over the top as far as the bling is concerned. I used to wear it to show it off, but now I enjoy seeing the reaction of folks when I allow them to hold it or wear it.

One night during the playoffs in 2017, I was wearing the ring while sitting by myself at a hotel bar in Houston. I was sipping a glass of Dry Riesling and watching a playoff game when an attractive woman who looked to be in her mid 40's approached me and asked if I was wearing a super bowl ring. When I informed her it was an NBA ring, she became even more curious. She asked if she could wear the ring and take a selfie with it. I said ok. When she handed the ring back to me she noticed the gold band on my left hand.

"Oh, you're married?" she asked. When I said yes, she responded, "Well, that's disappointing." I said, "It is?" She then finished her sentence, "...because I really think you'd be perfect...for my mom." Wow, so much for an ego boost! I then asked this lady how old her mom was and she said, "Oh, about your age. She's 64." Since I was only 58 I let her know that she was guilty of a punch below the belt. She actually felt bad about it and insisted on buying me a glass of wine before she returned to her friends. I allowed her to do so. After all, she should've known I was too young (and too married) for her mom. Although I suffered a momentary ego deflation, I did get a nice glass of German white wine and a story out of this encounter, and that was fine for me.

# The West Catholic Hall of Fame

In June of 2018, Gerry and I decided to attend a concert at the Woodlands (north of Houston) to see the Christian rock band, Third Day. On the drive over, two pretty cool things happened. Shortly after leaving Austin, I got several text messages informing me that my good friend Andrew Monaco had been named the play-by-play voice of the Texas A&M University Aggies. I had written a letter on Andrew's behalf but knew that over 200 applicants had expressed an interest in the position.

Andrew is not only a great guy but a versatile and hard-working broadcaster. I was thrilled for him. About an hour later, I got a call from Brian Fluck, the Head Football Coach at West Catholic High, my alma mater. Coach Fluck was on a committee to select inductees into the school's Sports Hall of Fame. I had been selected for induction and would be honored along with several fellow former athletes in October. I was very happy to hear the news, and my mind raced back to all those years being associated with West Catholic baseball.

It started when I was a batboy in the late '60s, a fan in the early '70s, and then a JV and varsity player. Playing for West was a source of pride for me. After struggling at the plate in my junior season, I came back strong. In my senior year, I hit .356 while starting every game at first base. I was awarded the team MVP trophy. Playing for West Catholic was the epitome for me. All those hours when I was young taking a few more hacks during batting practice or fielding extra ground balls at first base on bad-hop infields had paid off. I was in my school's sports hall of fame. The committee also mentioned my work as Sports Editor of the school yearbook and newspaper as well. It may have taken 41 years, but I appreciated the recognition.

*The West Catholic Sports Hall of Fame -- Class of 2018*

---

Usually when I write a song the lyrics come first and then I try to work in a melody. When I wrote "You Know Me Well" it was the opposite. I was taking a walk one day and this upbeat punchy melody kept dancing around in my brain. When I got home, I hummed the melody into my iPhone. A day or two later, I wrote all three verses and a chorus to the tune. When I took the song in the studio, producer Nic Whitworth changed up the tempo a bit and added a rocking piano, while trumpet player extraordinaire Fletch Wiley arranged the horn parts to bring the song all together and add some fullness to the entire production.

I was especially happy when legendary Austin vocalist Malford Milligan laid down a vocal track. Nic then mixed in Malford's parts with mine (female vocalists Meg Hays, Danielle Krieg, and Lindsey Dukes had already lent their considerable talents) I am of the opinion that if the right band or solo artist took a chance on "You Know Me Well," perhaps it could be a hit. Stranger things have happened.

---

***"You Know Me Well"***

*It's a middle of the day hey to let you know what I was thinking*

*I just gotta say without you I'd be sinking*

*Chorus*

*You know me well and I can tell it so*

*Gotta keep it going   moving in the right direction*

*I'm gonna keep on showing you some loving and affection*

*Repeat Chorus*

*Looking down the line now and seeing us together*

*Gone are the dark clouds   It's only getting better*

*Repeat Chorus*

---

## The Mitt

About a month after receiving the news that I was to be honored by West Catholic, I was at the Jersey Shore visiting my sister Peg's house for a little family get-together. Back when I was playing ball, I treated my first baseman's mitt like it was gold. It was my most prized possession. Shortly after high school graduation in 1977, my brother Tom (also a left-handed first baseman) asked if he could borrow the mitt since he was going to play in a softball league at Finnegan Playground. I lent him the glove, and then I went on to Temple University, the American Academy of Broadcasting, and then soon started my radio career.

I had totally forgotten about my mitt. The day before this family gathering in New Jersey in 2018, Tom had been cleaning out his garage, and at the bottom of a cardboard box tucked away in a corner, was my high school first baseman's mitt. He brought it the next day, and flipped it over to me, nonchalantly saying, "Oh here's your mitt back." It had only been 41 years since I had seen my old friend. I now keep the mitt in my garage, but I refuse to put it in a box, keeping it on a shelf so I can see it from time to time. I get the feeling the old mitt wants me to take it out and have a catch with it sometime. Just seeing that glove brings me back to a time when playing baseball was one of the most important aspects of my life.

## Kairos

In 2005 I had what might be best described as a "spiritual awakening." Although I had always been a believer, I had stopped attending church on a regular basis and was not raising my sons in the church. Professionally, things could not have been better for me in 2005. The Spurs had just won their second championship in three years, and I felt like I was at the peak of my career. However, I was becoming neglectful as a husband and father. Playing the horses, golfing, and listening to music with my friends was occupying much of my downtime and was pulling me away from home. One day I completely forgot I was supposed to take Karl to football practice because I had scheduled a tee time.

Things of this nature were happening more frequently, and I felt strongly that I needed to change my priorities. I knew deep down that I needed God in my life. Gerry and I took the boys with us as we visited various churches. Even though Gerry and I were raised in the Catholic Church, we were interested in a community of Christian faith, regardless of denomination. We visited Episcopal, Lutheran, Catholic, non-denominational, and Methodist churches. We felt at home when we visited Bethany

United Methodist. The folks there seemed authentic and open-minded, and the praise band was top-notch. Music is an important part of worship to me.

After a brief trial period, we decided to join Bethany and get involved. My NBA responsibilities and travel schedule make it difficult but I sing in the praise band at Bethany when I can. Gerry helps on Communion Sunday and serves as the treasurer for our Sunday School class. Getting plugged in with service-oriented Christians was good for both of us and probably saved our marriage. I still have fun with my friends, but there is much more balance in my life now.

In the spring of 2018, the Spurs had lost in the first round of the playoffs to Golden State, so I had a long off-season coming up. Gerry and I took a drive out the Big Bend National Park in far southwest Texas. While on a hiking trail, I told Gerry that I felt the need to help someone that summer. I just wasn't quite sure where I was needed. When we returned to the hotel I got a quick answer.

I received a call from church friend Randy Nettles, who plays guitar in Messengers of Grace, the praise band at Bethany. Randy was the music leader for a Kairos Weekend that July and needed a singer. Kairos is a four-day spiritual retreat for prison inmates. Forty-two "Brothers in White" take part in this particular program which is held at the Ferguson Unit of the Texas Department of Criminal Justice, just outside Madisonville in east Texas.

Randy's pitch to me was almost comical, "Hey, how would you like to spend four days in a Maximum Security State Prison with 42 criminals who are serving 25 years to life?" Even though it would've been easy to say no, I felt compelled to be part of this. I said yes almost immediately. Preparations included a handful of rehearsals as we practiced several dozen songs.

There was also a day of training at a TDCJ facility, and each volunteer was responsible for baking 100 dozen cookies. Each inmate at the unit receives a dozen cookies during the Kairos retreat, not just the 42 guys in the program. The responsibility of delivering those cookies to the inmates on the cell blocks fell on first-year volunteers. Since I was a rookie, I was scheduled to make the "cookie run" in cellblock H.

An inmate classified as a "trustee" named Chris would shadow me in the cellblock, which may have been the darkest place I've ever been. With no air conditioning, it was well over 90 degrees when Chris and I made our way into the cellblock. After a guard unlocked an outer gate and then an inner gate, and just before we started distributing the bags of cookies, Chris leaned over to my ear. "I just want to warn you, sir," he whispered, "We are now going into the real hood. There are some bad dudes down here." That wasn't exactly reassuring, but I was serving on a prison ministry team at a Maximum Security Unit. I wasn't expecting to encounter Boy Scouts.

As I handed these men a bag of cookies, I was surprised to find many of them gracious. Some even replied with a "God Bless You" after I greeted them that way. A few took the goodies without saying anything, while others were still sleeping, so we'd leave the cookies on their bed. The conditions were appalling. Two inmates were housed in each small cell, with bunk beds, a toilet and a sink. Some would hang a blanket over the toilet area to provide some semblance of privacy.

I saw several inmates take water from the toilet and splash it onto the concrete floor, then lay in that water in an effort to cool off. It was only 9 AM. How hot would it be out on the cellblock by late afternoon? I was only halfway through my distribution duties when I realized I needed a break. I was soaked with sweat, and I still had a full day of singing and fellowship ahead back in the chapel (which was air-conditioned). Chris walked me back to the chapel, and then he finished my rounds for me.

I gave myself an old-fashioned marine bath, tried to flap my shirt dry, and freshened up the best I could. I was bothered by the conditions I witnessed and felt like I needed to visit with the prison chaplain before returning to my role as singer in the band. I also needed to cool off a bit more. I told the chaplain that I couldn't see how the state of Texas could possibly rehabilitate offenders if they had to endure that kind of environment. He then stopped me and asked what cellblock I had been visiting.

When I told him Cellblock H, he responded that the state of Texas wasn't interested in rehabilitating those inmates, since most are serving life sentences and will never get back into society. I knew I was stepping out of my comfort zone to serve on this team, but this was eye-opening stuff. After I cooled down and had lunch back in the chapel, it was time to sing some songs and get the 42 Brothers in White up on their feet.

It was then that I saw God at work. In most prisons in this country, there is a racial divide. Out in the yard at the Ferguson Unit, the black, white and Hispanic inmates don't have a lot of interaction with each other. The first song after lunch that Saturday afternoon was "Lean on Me," which had been a hit in the early '70s for Bill Withers. As Randy and I began singing, I noticed something I hadn't seen before. The inmates were putting their arms around each other and singing out loud, not paying any attention to race.

We had rehearsed as a band several times, but I don't think we sounded nearly as good as we did that day. We were connecting with these guys, and they were embracing the song and the moment. I fought back tears as I watched this unfold. Later, when we broke into "Saints Come Marching In," the Brothers in

White, along with the volunteers, started to form a dance train. Every one of these guys was laughing, singing, and dancing.

Remember, most of them were serving long sentences and didn't really have much reason to laugh, sing or dance. When the song ended and as the applause started to die down, Randy leaned over to me and said, "That's the Holy Spirit right there." At that point, in July of 2018, in the middle of one of the toughest units in the Texas Department of Criminal Justice, I watched God shed sunlight on a very dark place. I went back to serve on another Kairos team at Ferguson in 2019 and witnessed God at work once again.

During these weekends, I had ample time to visit inmates and hear their stories. While it's easy for us to judge murderers, rapists, and robbers, there are also many reasons why they ended up committing those crimes and wound up in a place like Ferguson. Many were abused or neglected from a very young age. The words love, unity, and forgiveness were not part of their vocabulary growing up. I am thankful each day that I was part of a loving family and got lots of encouragement from my parents, friends, teachers and siblings. If ever there was a ministry that would humble me and remind me to be grateful for all that I'd been given, it would be the Kairos Prison Ministry.

*Jeff Border, me, Randy Nettles and Ron Lisle formed the band for the Kairos Prison Ministry in July of 2018. Playing and singing for the inmates was an emotional and spiritual experience for each of us.*

# 93

## Points Galore

The highest scoring basketball game I've ever called occurred on January 10th, 2019, as the San Antonio Spurs outlasted the Oklahoma City Thunder, 154-147 in double overtime. It was the highest combined score in the NBA since 2006. The eye-popping numbers were everywhere. The Spurs incredibly hit their first 14 three-pointers and ended up hitting 16 of 19 from beyond the arc, good for a percentage of 84.2%, an all-time NBA record for a team that had attempted at least 15 threes.

Russell Westbrook of the Thunder recorded a triple-double, which was nothing new for him but it included a career-high 24 assists. LaMarcus Aldridge of the Spurs scored a career-high 56 points, the most points ever scored by a Spur in the Gregg Popovich era.  Speaking of Pop, the win that evening was career win #1,222, as he surpassed Jerry Sloan for #3 on the all-time regular-season wins list. In the NBA, during the long 82 game grind, we often say the game that particular evening is just "1 of 82." The Spurs' win over the Thunder that night was anything but.

## 94

## Comebacks

With as many sporting events as I've seen as a fan and covered as a broadcaster, I've witnessed some pretty amazing comebacks. Fans that have listened to me for the past two decades on the Spurs Radio Network know that I wait until I am absolutely certain the game is in the win column before I say the Spurs can "put this one in the back pocket."

On June 8th, 1989, I had seats right behind the plate at the Vet in Philly as the Phillies hosted the Pirates. In the top of the 1st inning, the Pirates took no prisoners and scored 10 runs, three of them coming on a majestic home run by Barry Bonds. My five-year-old son Eric was very excited about being at the game so we decided to stick it out to see if the Phillies could at least score a few runs and make it interesting. They did exactly that, chipping away at the Pirates' lead.

The Phillies trailed 11-10 heading into the bottom of the 8th. Darren Daulton capped a rally with a two-run single and the Phillies ended up winning the game 15-11. Eric is now in his mid-thirties but remembers one aspect of the game vividly. The Phillies mascot, the Phanatic, made an appearance after the Pirates' 10-run first. He climbed on top of the dugout but had ace bandages wrapped around his entire body. He was walking with crutches and had his arm in a sling. It was as if he had taken the entire brunt of that ten-run rally.

After each inning when the Phillies scored, nibbling away at that ten-run lead, the Phanatic would re-emerge, and dramatically shed at least one item from his wounds. At first, it was the bandage around his head, then the sling, and finally when Daulton gave the home team the lead for good, the Phanatic threw away the crutch.

In the meantime, Pirates radio analyst Jim Rooker told his audience that if the Pirates blew a 10 run lead and lost the game he would walk the 320 miles back to Pittsburgh. He didn't walk back that night, but true to his word, as soon as the regular season concluded, Rooker began the trek from Philadelphia to Pittsburgh. He left the City of Brotherly Love on October 5th, and made it to the Steel City on October 17th, raising money for charity.

In 1986, the Sam Houston State Bearkats opened their brand new football stadium and had recorded a 5-0 record at home as they had a chance to win the Gulf Star Conference title and a berth in the NCAA Division 1-AA football playoffs. It was not looking good, however, in the regular-season finale. The Bobcats of Southwest Texas took a 31-10 lead into the fourth quarter and it looked like Sam Houston was going to lose at home for the first time in their new facility.

Quarterback Reggie Lewis and wide receiver Ricky Wolf had other ideas as Lewis hit Wolf for two fourth-quarter touchdowns and the Bearkats also converted on a critical two-point conversion and Sam Houston won the first-ever Gulf Star title with an amazing 32-31 victory. My broadcast partner for that game, Kooter Roberson, missed the entire comeback, as he was scheduled to call a New Waverly High School football playoff game in

Palestine, Texas that night. He left with Sam Houston trailing 31-10.

He listened to me on his way to the high school game, but the 1490 AM signal faded on him before he got to Palestine. He found out the final score when he called the station from the high school press box. After the game, Southwest Texas head coach John O'Hara told reporters that he felt like a "gutted snowbird." Whenever we referenced the game in the years that followed, we called it the "gutted snowbird game."

On December 9th, 2004 The Spurs played an early-season game at the Toyota Center against the Houston Rockets and led by ten points with less than a minute left in the fourth quarter. With :35 seconds remaining, Houston's 6'8" guard Tracy McGrady hit a three-pointer. It triggered an incredible example of individual late game heroics, as McGrady eventually scored 13 points in 35 seconds, and the Rockets had an improbable 81-80 win. Many Rockets fans missed McGrady's onslaught, as they had made their way to the exits during the fourth quarter. The good news for the Spurs is that they didn't allow that loss to bother them. They won nine of the next ten games, finished the season with a 59-23 record, and defeated Detroit in seven games in the NBA Finals to capture their third Larry O'Brien trophy.

In game one of the 2013 NBA western conference semifinals, the Spurs were not sharp at all. They looked out of rhythm at both ends of the floor, and guard Steph Curry of the Golden State Warriors was hitting from all over the floor. With four minutes remaining in regulation, the Spurs trailed by 16, and I was fully expecting to see Coach Popovich clear the bench, especially since Tim Duncan had to sit out the fourth quarter with a stomach flu.

Amazingly, the Warriors started turning the ball over and began missing shots, and the Spurs went on an 18-2 run to tie the game and send it into overtime. In the second overtime with the

Warriors leading by one, Manu Ginobili caught an inbounds pass on the left wing, and drained a three-pointer over a late-charging Curry with 1.2 seconds remaining, and the Spurs recorded a 129-127 double-overtime victory. The Spurs went on to win that series 4 games to 2, and there's little doubt that the tone was set with a remarkable comeback in Game 1.

## Milestones

I've been fortunate enough to watch or call some pretty amazing sports feats. On August 10th, 1981, I was in Philly on vacation and snagged a couple of tickets to see the Cardinals vs. Phillies game that evening. My buddy John Grego, who showed me the ropes at WKXK in Pana, Illinois two years earlier, had come to my hometown for a visit. Grego was a lifetime Cardinals fan, so there was some good-natured ribbing going on as we went to Veterans Stadium that warm evening. Grego and I were part of a crowd of 60,000 to see Pete Rose record his 3,631st hit, surpassing Cardinal great Stan Musial, for most hits in the history of the National League. Musial was in attendance that evening. Ironically, when Musial got the last hit of his Hall of Fame career 18 years earlier, it was a single that went past a Cincinnati rookie second baseman by the name of Pete Rose.

On June 5th, 1993 the Texas Longhorn baseball team took on Oklahoma State in a first-round matchup at the College World Series in Omaha. With Texas junior All-America and two-time National Player of the Year Brooks Kieschnick on the mound, the largest single-game crowd in CWS history (over 20,000) was on hand to watch a battle between two traditional college baseball powers. In all my years of playing, watching, and covering baseball, I can honestly say I never saw a more intense competitor than Kieschnick. I have always said he played baseball like a middle linebacker.

He was an outstanding hitter but was also the #1 starter on the mound. At 6'4 and 230 pounds, he cut an imposing figure, and he brought a 15-3 pitching record to Omaha. In the ninth inning of the Oklahoma State game, with the Horns clinging to a 6-5 lead, Kieschnick had gone the distance but had already thrown over 150 pitches. When OSU began a ninth-inning rally, Coach Cliff Gustafson ambled his way out to the mound to check on Kieschnick. He had two relievers ready to go in the bullpen.

The look on Kieschnick's face said it all - he was not about to give that ball to Gus. He was going to finish this game no matter what. Sure enough, Kieschnick averted further danger and recorded the final out with his 11th strikeout, and the Horns advanced in the winner's bracket. The final official pitch count was 172- the most pitches I had ever seen thrown by a pitcher in a single game. After the win, Coach Gus told the assembled media, "I just announced to the team that Kieschnick will be the starter for Monday's game since he didn't throw that many pitches tonight."

In 1994, the Longhorn football team hosted the fifth-ranked Colorado Buffaloes and their Heisman trophy candidate, running back Rashaan Salaam. Despite fighting cramps in his back throughout the course of the game, Salaam knifed his way through the Longhorn defense and rushed for 317 yards in a 34-31 Colorado victory. It was the most rushing yards surrendered by the Horns in 102 years of Texas football, and the second-highest total in Colorado history. Salaam went on to rush for 2,055 yards that season, becoming only the fourth running back in college history to rush for over 2000 yards. His outstanding campaign earned him the Heisman Trophy. Four seasons later, I had the privilege of describing Ricky Williams' incredible season, which included 2,124 rushing yards and 27 touchdowns. Williams, like Salaam, also won the Heisman.

In an earlier story, I mentioned Major Applewhite's record-setting night against the Washington Huskies in the 2001 Holiday Bowl in San Diego. It was my final Longhorn broadcast (since I had already started with the Spurs) and the Horns trailed by as many as 19. The Huskies led 36-20 entering the fourth quarter. Applewhite engineered four touchdown drives in the fourth quarter and finished the night with 473 passing yards, a school record, in a heart-stopping 47-43 win. It was a sweet way to cap off my 12 years on the Longhorn Radio Network.

On February 21st, 2007, The Spurs played a road game at Atlanta. The Spurs opened up a large lead in the first half thanks to guard Manu Ginobili. I had never seen, and don't think I ever will see again an individual player score 24 straight points. He scored on twisting layups, pull-up mid-range jumpers, three-pointers, and he hit seven of seven free throws during the flurry. He finished with 40 points in a 103-96 Spurs win. Atlanta television analyst Steve Smith, who was a teammate of Ginobili's during Manu's rookie year, said the performance was "Jordan Like." On the radio, I just called it "Manu Voodoo."

During my seasons with the Spurs, I have witnessed many incredible feats. The Spurs big three of Tim Duncan, Manu Ginobili and Tony Parker played together for fourteen seasons, and together captured 4 NBA titles, 575 regular season and 126 playoff victories, making them the winningest trio in modern NBA history. The '80s Lakers trio featuring Magic Johnson, Kareem Abdul Jabbar and James Worthy combined for three titles while Boston's threesome of Larry Bird, Kevin McHale and Robert Parrish also won three rings, but the Spurs' Big Three not only won four titles together, but they were instrumental in a run that allowed the Spurs to establish an all-time NBA record that will likely never be equaled. For 18 consecutive seasons, the Spurs won at least 50 regular-season games. The previous mark (held by the Showtime Lakers) had been 12 seasons. I consider myself very fortunate to have been along for the ride.

# All 50 Club

Maybe it's because I grew up in the inner city, but I always had a fascination with nature and wide-open spaces. Other than an Amtrak train trip to Florida in early 1978, I had never ventured outside the four-state region of Pennsylvania, New Jersey, Delaware and New York. When I accepted my first radio gig at WKXK in Pana, Illinois in April of 1979, I boarded a plane for the first time. I remember thinking during that maiden voyage that perhaps one day I'd be lucky enough to fly to cities and broadcast games from all over the country.

If I was really fortunate, maybe I could join the All 50 Club, spending time in each of the 50 states. When the opportunities to travel for work came my way a few years later, I was elated. I would always try to book early flights departing and later flights returning so I could maximize my time at these new locales. My six years broadcasting for Sam Houston State enhanced my belief that one day I could make it to all 50.

The Sam Houston basketball team usually traveled by motorcoach throughout the south, while the football team had a tendency to head west. With the move up to Division 1-AA in football, the schedule included games at Nevada-Reno, Boise

State, and Montana State. When the Bearkats played at Montana State in 1987, I drove my rental car south after the game to Yellowstone Park, just so I could cross Wyoming off the list.

It was early evening and the park was about to close, but I convinced the Park Ranger that I just needed to drive into the park a few miles and would be back in 10-15 minutes. I was so tempted to drive far into the park to observe this beautiful place, but I kept my word, vowing to myself to one day return. Years later, I got to spend time hiking at Yellowstone and the Grand Tetons. The most scenic drive I have ever taken starts at Jackson Hole, north through the two national parks and into Paradise Valley in southern Montana.

When I started broadcasting games for the University of Texas in three different sports, I was traveling nine months out of the year. In the NBA, we travel to 29 cities coast to coast. By the summer of 2012, my eleventh season with the Spurs, I was lacking only Alaska and North Dakota. I knocked off North Dakota when Gerry and I hiked in the Teddy Roosevelt National Park, the most remote of the two dozen parks we have visited. It's outside Medora, in the far western part of North Dakota.

In the summer of 2013, I got to #50 when we sailed on an Alaskan Cruise. Wisely, we added the train ride and two-day stay at Denali National Park. On one of our excursions, six folks from our ship joined us on a whitewater raft ride on the Nenah River. The "captain" of our raft asked where everyone was from. When Gerry and I said Texas, he responded, "Texas? I could never live there. I'd get claustrophobic."

## Streak Stopper

I got an early wake-up call on Halloween Day, 1998. I was staying at the Cornhusker Inn in downtown Lincoln and I was scheduled to speak to the Big Red Booster Club at their breakfast. Hours later, the Longhorns would take the field in front of 76,000 Cornhusker fans on a cold, gray Nebraska Saturday afternoon. The Cornhuskers had invited me to be the guest speaker and I couldn't believe the size of my audience. I looked out over a hotel ballroom full of red-clad Husker fans. There must've been 300 in attendance.

After my ten-minute speech, I opened it up for questions and I could tell that these folks had respect for Texas, but really didn't expect much of a game. After all, the 7th ranked Cornhuskers had won 47 in a row at Memorial Stadium, which was the fifth-best home streak in NCAA history. Nebraska was also home of the "blackshirts," one of the best defenses in the nation.

The unranked Longhorns relied on their standout running back Ricky Williams, but it had been ten seasons since an opposing running back gained over 100 yards in Lincoln. On this day, however, Texas was determined to give it to Williams early and often, and the eventual Heisman Trophy winner tallied 150 yards on 37 carries, redshirt freshman Major Applewhite played the quarterback position like a gym rat point guard.

He was tough and gritty and absorbed several huge hits while completing passes to six different receivers for 269 yards in a hard-fought 20-16 win. The Horns' defense was also stellar that day, coming up with key stops. As the players were leaving Tom Osborn Field, many of the Cornhusker faithful stayed to cheer on the visiting team, some of them chanting "Heisman" in honor of Ricky. It had been seven seasons since these fans saw an opposing team walk off that field with a win. It may have been the classiest display of sportsmanship by a fan base that I have seen in my career.

# "Here Comes Smokin' Joe"

As I previously mentioned, I originally wrote "Here Comes Smokin' Joe" for a documentary that never was produced, but it was important for me to follow through and finish the tribute to my favorite boxer. Joe Frazier started in very humble beginnings as the son of a sharecropper in rural Beaufort, South Carolina. If ever there was an example of a self-made man and the American dream, look no further than Smokin' Joe Frazier.

***"Here Comes Smokin' Joe"***

*Walking down these streets*

*Feeling good today*

*Finding his own beat*

*Now he's on his way*

*As he starts to wander all around this town*

*He feels the Philly rhythm*

*All that's going down*

*Chorus*

*Here Comes Smokin' Joe*

*left hooks he is throwing*

*Climbing up the ranks*

*to the title he is going*

*Can't forget his youth*

*Those hours in the sun*

*Lessons that will last until the fight is done*

*As you start to ponder the legends of the ring*

*Don't forget Joe Frazier*

*heart and toughness he would bring*

*Repeat Chorus*

# A Lost Night in Mexico City

On December 4th, 2013 the Spurs were scheduled to play the Minnesota Timberwolves in an NBA Global Games contest at the Mexico City arena. We had ventured to Mexico City for a preseason game in 2009, but this was a regular-season game to be played in a brand new, state-of-the-art arena that had been built in 2012.

About two hours prior to the game, while visiting with former Spurs guard Terry Porter (at the time an assistant coach with Minnesota) we noticed some smoke near the rafters. For a brief time, players continued going through their pregame warm-ups, but soon the smoke got thicker and we were all asked to leave the arena bowl until officials could determine the origin of the smoke. Apparently, a generator malfunction caused a fire that filled the arena with a thick haze. It looked like a Cheech and Chong movie. There was no way the game could be played.

A sellout crowd of 20,000 folks, most of whom never entered the arena, was sent home. The Spurs traveling party started to head back to the Mexico City Airport, but the traffic around the arena was congested and that ride took forever. Upon arriving at the airport, we had to wait several hours to board our plane, because the crew wasn't expecting to fly until midnight. The flight back to Texas was uneventful until we were told that there were no customs agents available in San Antonio, so we would have to fly to Dallas, and then return to San Antonio.

There were not many happy campers on the charter. When we arrived in Dallas, it was around 5 am, and we had to traverse most of the DFW airport to go through the customs process. At one point, I remember an escalator ride. I was a few feet behind Matt Bonner, and just in front of Matt was Tim Duncan. The adjacent escalator was going down, while we were going up. I overheard a young man tell his friend as we were passing, "Dude, I swear that was Matt Bonner!" At that point, I laughed out loud. I love Matt and consider him a good friend, but those guys didn't notice the Hall of Famer on the step above him!

At that point, I was probably delirious from the lack of sleep. As we finally got close to our charter it seemed as if we had toured the entire airport with countless security checks and it was now daylight. Assistant Coach Jim Boylan, who later became the head coach of the Chicago Bulls, looked over at me and just shook his head in frustration. I told him, "Don't fret Jim, it's just one more story for the book." At the time, I didn't really know if I would ever write a book, but since I've written one now I feel compelled to share the story of the worst trip in my two decades with the Spurs.

## 100

## Cruising the Rhine

Since I've enjoyed so many wonderful excursions both professionally and personally, I didn't want to end the book on a bad trip, but instead with my favorite trip ever. In the summer of 2017, Gerry and I splurged and decided to take the Viking River Cruise from Amsterdam to Basel, Switzerland. It was a glorious eight days. After two days in Amsterdam (which included a tour of the Anne Frank House and a trip to the Rijksmuseum where we saw original works by Van Gogh and Rembrandt), we headed down the Rhine.

From windmills in Kinderdijk, Holland to the 800-year-old Marksburg Castle in Braubach, Germany, to the WWII battlefields in Alsace in eastern France, the entire trip was educational and exhilarating. We learned much about the food, culture and history of different cities and countries. I got to practice mein schlechtes Deutsch (my bad German) and the French and German wines served on the ship at night put an exclamation point on each day. The memories of those eight days will stay with both of us for a long time.

## A few extras while I got ya...

A few extras while I got ya...

True confession - I was going to stop at 100 stories because that seemed like a good cutoff point, but then I thought of a few more and I didn't want to hurt their feelings by not including them.

On February 7th, 2001 the Texas Longhorn basketball team went to Boulder and defeated the Colorado Buffaloes, 77-72. Following the game, CU Sports information director Dave Plati asked me for a quick favor. Knowing that I do a pretty decent impersonation of legendary Chicago Cubs announcer Harry Caray, Plati wanted me to call former Colorado Head Football Coach Rick Neuheisel and wish him a happy 40th birthday. Neuheisel at the time was heading up the University of Washington football program, where his star quarterback was Marques Tuiasosopo.

As I left the message in Neuheisel's mailbox, I made sure to totally botch the pronunciation of both his name and that of his quarterback (in typical Harry fashion). The message went something like, "Hey Coach Newhoozle, this is Harry Caray in

Chicago calling to wish you a happy 40th birthday. I really like your team, especially that quarterback Marques Tooiapapoopoo. Have a great one Coach Newheezle." The following day Plati informed me that he had gotten a brief phone message from Neuheisel saying, "Who the HELL was that?"

In October 2008 I was invited to play in a charity golf tournament at a Par 3 Course in Austin called Butler Pitch and Putt. On the 88 yard 4th hole, I hit a pitching wedge that landed on the green and one-hopped into the cup for my first (and only) hole-in-one. My fellow playing partners were just as excited as I was. There was a sign adjacent to the tee box declaring that a Hole-in-One wins a trip to a golf resort in Canada. Thanks to that lucky bounce, Gerry and I got to spend four days and nights at the Algonquin Hotel and Resort in St. Andrews By the Sea, New Brunswick, Canada. It's an overused cliche,' but sometimes it's true- it really is better to be lucky than good!

In 2009 I was asked to be the guest speaker at the Northwest Hills United Methodist Church for their annual men's steak dinner. I had spoken to every group imaginable, from the Kiwanis to the Rotary, so I had plenty of stories for the 20-minute time slot and accepted the invitation. The church member who recruited me was a big sports fan and very familiar with my work. When I arrived for the dinner I was surprised by the size of the gymnasium/fellowship hall and also stunned by the huge screen at the end of the gym with a picture of me and a list of my "accomplishments."

Pastor Bill Henderson greeted me warmly and thanked me for agreeing to speak. Seizing an opportunity, I then thanked the Pastor for finding room in his budget to accommodate my fee. The look on his face was priceless. For a moment, he didn't know I was kidding. Within a few somewhat awkward seconds, I assured the good Pastor that this was a freebie, but I was definitely going to enjoy one of those steak dinners.

On February 7th, 2014 the Spurs were in New York for a game with the Brooklyn Nets. After the 103-89 loss, I went to my favorite watering hole in midtown Manhattan, PJ Clarke's, which was founded in 1884. During World War II, songwriter Johnny Mercer wrote a song while sitting at PJ Clarke's. "One For My Baby" became a hit for Frank Sinatra. The opening line of the song is "It's quarter to three…no one in the place except you and me ." Since I was in the city that never sleeps, I found myself still hanging at 2:45 AM, a quarter to three. Therefore, I made certain that the jukebox selection was "One For My Baby." There were still about a dozen patrons remaining and several of us chimed in for an impromptu sing along. I'm still not certain if this sort of behavior is nerdy or cool, perhaps a little of both.

During the 2019-20 NBA season, the Spurs traveled to New Orleans for a game with the Pelicans. On all road games, Spurs Radio hires a local statistician who is compensated for providing me numbers pertinent to the action. Even though we have stat monitors at our broadcast locations, statisticians can compile and share complimentary numbers, such as individual points in a quarter or team turnovers in a half, etc. For this particular game, a new statistician was assigned to me. I can't remember his name, but I believe he was a college kid. He was a very pleasant fellow. During the first timeout he slipped me a piece of paper saying the Spurs had hit 3 of their first 8 shots and were shooting 33%. Trust me, I am far from a wizard in arithmetic, but I informed him that 3 of 9 would be 33%. He then, very nonchalantly, said, "Oh, Bill, I meant to tell you, I'm really not good at math." I needed this guy to be good at one thing and one thing only - MATH!

In the spring of 2021, I called a handful of college baseball games at NCAA Division II St. Edward's University in Austin. I had missed broadcasting baseball and was looking forward to getting a few games in. My broadcast position was just outside the main press box under a large blue tent, just a few yards away from some fans sitting in lawn chairs. I did a solo broadcast on the half dozen games I called for St. Edward's that season.

Just prior to the Lubbock Christian game, public address announcer Justin Simmons welcomed the crowd (perhaps 150 strong) and informed the fans that the game could be heard on The Lone Star Conference Digital Network with the "legendary" Bill Schoening. For just a moment, I allowed my chest to puff up. Seconds later, a lady sitting in one of those lawn chairs looked over at me and said, "Bill who?" I responded by shrugging my shoulders, telling the lady I never heard of him either!

# Epilogue

Well, there you have it. Thanks so much for taking the time to read a few of the stories that have shaped my life. I have been so incredibly blessed to have been able to follow my dream, and have the support of a brilliant woman. Gerry has literally taken care of everything, which has allowed me to focus on being the best play-by-play guy I can be. We've been fortunate to have two sons who are both successful, caring, loving people and I'm proud of them both personally and professionally.

While I was writing this book, a dark cloud descended upon our country raining down racism, hatred, violence, and division. That cloud has been hovering for way too long. It's my vow to always do what I can to promote the opposite - harmony, love, peace, and unity. I hope you've enjoyed some of the stories I've included here. From the Schoening home office in Austin, Texas —Goodnight everybody!

Eric, Bill, Gerry, and Karl Schoening

# Acknowledgments

Many Thanks.....

First and foremost to the Good Lord above, who has blessed me with an incredible life full of amazing people and experiences.

There are lots of folks to whom I owe a great deal of appreciation, including my late parents (Bill and Peggy Schoening) for their nurturing and love, my siblings (Peg, Liz, Tom, and Chris) for their nonstop encouragement, my wife Gerry for her faith in me from the start, and for accompanying me on this wild radio adventure, and my sons Eric and Karl for making their old man proud every day.

I'm also grateful for the men and women who gave me opportunities in my career. Richard Prather (WKXK), Dorothy Haney (KPET), Ray Eller (KSAM), Tom Dore (KLBJ), Ron Rogers (KVET), Andrew Ashwood (WOAI) and Lawrence Payne (San Antonio Spurs). I will be forever indebted to my musical friends Nic Whitworth and Mike Vasquez, who have been instrumental (see what I did there?) in helping me shape my songs and bring them to life. I'd also like to acknowledge the broadcast engineers, studio producers, media relations personnel, and statisticians with whom I've worked. Their behind-the-scene efforts help on-air guys like me look good (most of the time, anyway!) A special thanks to my longtime studio producer Mike Bartlett, who brings energy and a positive attitude each night, which isn't always easy during an 82 game season. Mike also helped edit my audio book. A special thanks to Renee Youngblood, who helped edit my early manuscript when this book was in its formative stages. I'd also like to acknowledge Spurs super fan Jane Ann Craig, who has taken many photos through the years, some of which made their way into this book. Finally, I'd like to thank my listeners. Television has long been the most popular way for fans to experience sporting events, but radio has been a constant companion for those who are in their car or can't make it to a screen to watch the game. I'm appreciative to those who tune in to just catch the score or listen to an entire broadcast.

## About the Author

Bill Schoening was born and raised in Philadelphia and had the good fortune to grow up right around the corner from a large playground, Finnegan Recreation Center. His childhood years spent playing a variety of sports instilled a deep love for athletics. Inspired by Phillies announcer Byrum Saam, the 10 year old Schoening decided he wanted to be a radio sportscaster. Ten years later, just a few days after graduating from the American Academy of Broadcasting, Schoening began his career in Pana, a small town in Central Illinois. He was able to broadcast some high school and junior college games, but on a very limited basis. He then accepted an offer to broadcast high school games at KPET in Lamesa, Texas. The station's strong commitment to sports gave Schoening the opportunity to call lots of games and work on his craft. Three years later, he was named the Play by Play voice at Sam Houston State in Huntsville, Texas. His duties at KSAM Radio in Huntsville also included covering the Texas Prison system, and he was the Texas Associated Press correspondent for 29 lethal injections. After six years in Huntsville, he was hired by KLBJ in Austin, where he got to work for Lady Bird Johnson and cover the University of Texas Longhorns. During his twelve years on the Longhorn Radio Network, Schoening called three College World Series, nine NCAA basketball tournaments, and the career of a Heisman trophy winner (Ricky Williams). In 2001, the San Antonio Spurs offered Schoening the chance to join the professional ranks. During his time behind the microphone, the Spurs have won four championships. Schoening's favorite hobby is songwriting, and has penned over two dozen songs, and has independently released three CD's of original music. He and wife Gerry live in Austin and have two adult sons, Eric and Karl.

www.ingramcontent.com/pod-product-compliance
Lightning Source LLC
Chambersburg PA
CBHW072148070526
44585CB00015B/1043